D0359368

CLASSIC CATHOLIC CONVERTS

FATHER CHARLES P. CONNOR

CLASSIC
CATHOLIC
CONVERTS

IGNATIUS PRESS   SAN FRANCISCO

The converts on the cover are
Elizabeth Ann Seton, G. K. Chesterton,
John Henry Newman, Ronald Knox,
and Edith Stein

Cover design by Riz Boncan Marsella

© 2001 Ignatius Press, San Francisco
All rights reserved
ISBN 978–0–89870–787–8
Library of Congress control number 00–100233
Printed in the United States of America ∞

In memory of my Mother

Alice C. Connor

whose Catholic faith
would inspire
any convert

THE AUTHOR ACKNOWLEDGES HIS
DEEP GRATITUDE TO

BARBARA QUINN

WHOSE PAINSTAKING WORK
FIRST BROUGHT THIS MANUSCRIPT
TO LIGHT

CONTENTS

FOREWORD

The Fathers of the Second Vatican Council in their Decree on Ecumenism wrote that "it is evident that the work of preparing and reconciling those individuals who wish for full Catholic communion is of its nature distinct from ecumenical action. But there is no opposition between the two, since both proceed from the marvellous ways of God."[1]

Father Charles Connor's *Classic Catholic Converts* might very well have been titled *Marvellous Ways of God* as understood by the Council Fathers.

Central to the Council's understanding of ecumenism is the Catholic's duty "to make a careful and honest appraisal of whatever needs to be renewed and done in the Catholic household itself, in order that its life may bear witness more clearly and faithfully to the teachings and institutions which have been handed down from Christ through the apostles".[2]

Classic Catholic Converts narrates the coming to Catholicism of brilliant intellectuals and religious foundresses, of authors and artists, of political personalities, scientists, and business people. These stories are indeed about individuals finding faith. They are also, however, glorious instances of accomplishing "whatever needs to be renewed and done in the Catholic household itself".

The personal influence, teaching, and example of the Catholic men and women who attracted these converts to Catholicism, as well as the lives of the converted themselves,

[1] Vatican II, *Unitatis Reintegratio*, no. 4, November 21, 1964.
[2] Ibid.

shine forth as both an appraisal and accomplishment of a renewed Catholic household. Marvellous ways of God, indeed. Ecumenism and an individual's full Catholic communion differ, and yet the essential of the former is found in the latter.

Walker Percy, author and convert to Catholicism, once wrote to a new convert, "Well, welcome. It is a very untidy outfit you're hooking up with." Father Connor's *Classic Catholic Converts*, so astutely presented here, completes that observation by forcefully reminding us that, when individuals find the Church, a "tidying up" occurs, a renewal in Christ's Body, the primary task in all ecumenical endeavors.

+ Most Reverend John M. Dougherty, D.D., V.G.
Auxiliary Bishop of Scranton

INTRODUCTION

In his *Confessions*, Saint Augustine of Hippo tells us that a
crucial stage in his conversion occurred when he was told of
others' paths to the Faith as well as of their lives in the Faith.
He writes: "After Simplicianus recounted the life of Vic-
torinus, I was on fire to follow his example—which is why he
had told me the story."

"Conversion" is a particularly arduous subject on which to
write. The author is charged with no small task, because he
must record things unutterable: the stirring of souls by the
Holy Spirit. To write aptly of conversion, an author must do
three things simultaneously. First, he must introduce a character searching for the truth. Second, he must explain how the
truth became evident and induced conversion. And third,
he must illustrate the effects of conversion. Father Charles
Connor succeeds on all three levels.

In this cogent and concise volume, Father Connor depicts
a plethora of men and women who searched for the truth,
found it, and, as the saying goes, "lived happily ever after",
that is, happily ever after in striving to follow the Lord Jesus
Christ. Though each story of conversion may share these
common elements, Father Connor's book is quick to show
that no two stories are quite alike. To be sure, each of the
conversions recounted herein is unique—unique in the prior
disposition of each soul, unique in the effects of grace upon
each soul.

Whom do we meet in Father Connor's book? We meet so
many converts as to make the book an embarrassment of

riches—an embarrassment of the riches of God's grace. Let me make mention of but two of the multitude of converts to whom Father Connor introduces us: Edith Stein and Dorothy Day. Contemporaries on either side of the Atlantic, these two women illustrate not only the different backgrounds, cultures, and journeys of so many converts but also the singular effect of the power of the Holy Spirit upon individual persons in their striving to live out fruitfully their transformation in the Faith.

Edith Stein came to the Faith from the academy in Germany. After a brilliant university career under the tutelage of the renowned philosopher Edmund Husserl, Edith took the Carmelite habit as Sister Teresa Benedicta of the Cross. The Holy Spirit called her to a life of prayer and sacrifice in the silence and solitude of the cloister. However, the horrors of Nazism wrenched her from her cloister, and her brief earthly life was offered up to God as a holocaust in the fires of Auschwitz.

Dorothy Day came to faith from the slums of America. After a tumultuous and disordered life of protest and political activism, Dorothy founded the Catholic Worker Movement. The Holy Spirit called her to a life of prayer and sacrifice in the hustle and bustle of the street. For the rest of her life, Dorothy was to live as a faithful Catholic in a constant effort to actualize the Church's preferential option for the poor on the streets of New York.

What heart can but be touched by the lives of the like of Edith Stein or Dorothy Day? Father Connor presents their stories, along with so many others, in such ways that we cannot, whether within or outside the Church, be moved. The annals of these many converts enrich each of us. The embarrassment of riches made manifest herein is worthwhile reading for any and all. For those who possess the Faith and for those who seek it, much is to be gained in keeping company with these historic converts. As the Church prays in the first Preface of Holy Men and Women in the Sacramentary, the "great company of witnesses spurs us onto victory, to share their prize of everlasting glory, through Jesus Christ our Lord".

In the following pages, Father Connor takes his lead from Saint Simplicianus, the ancient bishop of Milan and tutor of Saint Ambrose, who illuminated the Faith for the young Augustine through the lives of the saints. Father Connor recounts the conversion of numerous men and women to us, not merely as historical yarns, but as portraits of what we might one day be. He deftly succeeds in fanning the flame of faith—which is why he tells us these stories.

May I conclude this review by thanking Father Michael Hull, professor at Saint Joseph's Seminary, for his invaluable assistance.

+ John Cardinal O'Connor
Archbishop of New York
November 23, 1999

ELIZABETH ANN SETON

First American-born saint

Elizabeth Bayley Seton, the first native-born citizen of the United States to be canonized a saint, was of English ancestry and grew up in a family that had settled in colonial New York. Her father, Dr. Richard Bayley, was a physician; her mother, Catherine Charlton, the daughter of an Anglican minister. Together they had three daughters: Mary, Elizabeth, and Catherine. After Catherine's birth, Mrs. Bayley died, and some time later Dr. Bayley married Charlotte Barclay. Though primarily she was English, Charlotte Barclay's mother was also Dutch, a Roosevelt. Hence, through her stepmother, Elizabeth had a connection with both Presidents Roosevelt. She was also the aunt of a future archbishop of Baltimore, James Roosevelt Bayley.

Elizabeth was born August 28, 1774, on the eve of the American Revolution. Raised in the Episcopalian faith, she was by all accounts a strikingly beautiful young woman. Trinity Church, Wall Street, very close to the present New York Stock Exchange, was in the late eighteenth century the spiritual nucleus of the city, drawing its social and cultural elite together. Elizabeth knew this fashionable world very well, and when she married William Magee Seton on January 25, 1794, she married into a society to which she was accustomed. She and her husband, a prominent partner in a merchant shipping firm, had a fashionable wedding, and, after living with the Setons for some time, moved into their own home, Number 27 Wall Street. The contrast between Elizabeth's and William's attitude toward religion is interesting:

> She was earnest, sincere, only just sacramental, a Bible reader with a marked evangelical streak. Her husband, not very religious . . . belonged to a new breed of men. Today we would label him as an executive. For him trade came first.[1]

She, then, was the religious one. There does not appear to be any time in her life when Elizabeth lacked devotion, but in her married adult years her spiritual formation was greatly developed by a twenty-five-year-old High-Church curate serving at Trinity, John Henry Hobart, a scholarly man whose dynamic preaching bespoke conviction and deep spirituality. Hobart was the youngest of three associate ministers assisting Benjamin Moore, the rector of Trinity Church.

Hobart was described by one biographer as a man who "was short, disproportioned and wore thick spectacles".[2] He had met John Henry Newman in England, and the convert cardinal had been impressed with his intelligence. Elizabeth Seton and her sister-in-law Rebecca were two parishioners at Trinity who particularly came under his spell. In Elizabeth's case, Hobart had a complex personality to deal with:

> Betty had amassed an amazing hodgepodge of belief and observance. Thus she wore a Catholic crucifix, looked kindly

[1] Bernard Basset, S.J., *Saint Elizabeth Seton* (London: Catholic Truth Society, 1975), 4.

[2] Joseph I. Dirvin, C.M., *Mrs. Seton: Foundress of the American Sisters of Charity*, New Canonization Edition (New York: Farrar, Straus and Giroux, 1962, 1975), 84.

on the life of the cloister, subscribed to the doctrine of angels, liked Methodist hymns, the quietism of the Quakers and the emotionalism of Rousseau, read general Protestant works, practiced meditation, was inclined to the narrow Calvinism of her ancestors in the matter of sin and punishment, and attended the Episcopal Church.[3]

Despite her complexity, or perhaps because of it, the two had an almost immediate spiritual attraction. Elizabeth Seton was in love with God, and Henry Hobart was the man charged in God's providence with bringing this love to a higher earthly potential.

Not surprisingly, John Henry Hobart and his wife (who was the daughter of the minister who had officiated at the wedding of Elizabeth's parents) were frequent visitors at the home of the Setons.

A letter Elizabeth wrote to a friend, Julia Scott (delivered by Hobart himself), gives us an even better glimpse of what Elizabeth thought of Hobart:

The bearer of this letter possesses *in full* the reality of the last description in *my heart.* . . . The soother and comforter of the troubled *soul* is a kind of friend not often met with. The convincing, pious and singular turn of mind and argument possessed by this most amiable being has made him—without even having the least consciousness that he is so—the friend most my friend in this world, and one of those who, after my Adored Creator, I expect to receive the largest share of happiness from in the next.[4]

Some time later, because of the financial reversals of William Seton, the family moved from Wall Street to Number 8 State Street, a house at the geographical tip of Manhattan

[3] Ibid.
[4] Elizabeth Seton to Julia Scott, cited in ibid., 103.

Island, with panoramic views of the river and the bay. Long Island was to the east, New Jersey to the west, and Staten Island to the south. (Today, Our Lady of the Rosary shrine church is located here.)

In 1802, William Seton's health began to fail, and he was encouraged to go to a climate more conducive to his recovery. Leghorn (Livorno), Italy, was chosen because, among other reasons, it was the home of the Filicchi family, old friends and business associates of William Seton. Filippo was the head of the Filicchi firm. His wife, Mary Cowper, was from Boston, and through marriage and the prestige of his own business firm, he had become very well acquainted with the United States. He was on friendly terms with such patriots as Washington, Jefferson, and Madison, and he also knew John Carroll of Baltimore, the nation's first Catholic bishop. As proof of the esteem in which he was held, Filippo served as United States consul at Leghorn, most unusual for a native Italian. Filippo's brother, Antonio, was also a partner in the firm. His beautiful and charming wife, Amabilia, was to become very close to Elizabeth Seton.

The Filicchis were devout Catholics, though it is not known if in religious matters they ever made any impression on William Seton. William died in Italy in December 1803, and he is buried in the Protestant cemetery in Leghorn.

When the grace of Elizabeth's conversion began to crystallize is not clear. It is almost certain, though, that it began while she lived in Italy; there is nothing to indicate any strong attraction to the Catholic Church before, while she was still in New York.

We do know that while in Italy she would go frequently with the Filicchis to the Shrine of Our Lady of Montenaro in Leghorn. We also know that on a trip to Florence, she went to visit the cathedral (the Duomo), the Church of San Lorenzo,

Santa Maria Novella, and the Medici Chapel and that she was absolutely fascinated with their beauty.

Some time later she wrote to a friend:

> How happy would we be, if we believed what these dear souls believe: that they *possess* God in the Sacrament, and that He remains in their churches and is carried to them when they are sick! O, my! . . . how happy would I be, even so far away from all so dear, if I could find You in the church as they do . . . how many things I would say to You of the sorrows of my of my heart and the sins of my life! [5]

Her praying so intently to God that she might find Him seems strongly indicative that she wanted to believe in the Catholic doctrine of the Real Presence.

Elizabeth began to confide in her friends the Filicchis, and they provided her with books, all of which she read thoroughly. We know that she read Francis de Sales' *Introduction to the Devout Life*, a polemical work called *The Unerring Authority of the Catholic Church*, Bossuet's *Exposition of Catholic Doctrine*, and an orderly, step-by-step development of the Church's history, compiled and handwritten by Filippo with help from a priest friend, Father Pecci.

Elizabeth returned, finally, to New York City, very strongly leaning toward Catholicism. On the lengthy sea crossing she traveled with Antonio Filicchi. He had given her Butler's *Lives of the Saints*, which she read voraciously. In addition, they practically made a retreat—praying, fasting, and observing feast days with particular devotion.

Her greatest undoing in New York came when she let people know of her interest in Catholicism. Basing their questions most often on their own superficial prejudices, they

---

[5] Elizabeth Seton, cited in ibid., 137.

fired an incessant barrage of hostile queries at her. Elizabeth's former mentor, John Henry Hobart, was no less critical:

> When I see a person whose sincere and ardent piety I have always thought worthy of imitation in danger of connecting herself with a communion which my sober judgment tells me is a corrupt and sinful communion, I cannot be otherwise than deeply affected. . . . If it should appear that you have forsaken the religion of your forefathers, not from prejudices of education, not for want of better information, but in opposition to light and knowledge which few have enjoyed, my soul anxiously inquires, what answer will you make to your Almighty Judge? [6]

Hobart lost no time in providing Elizabeth Seton with a copy of Thomas Newton's famous book *Dissertation on the Prophesies*, the main thesis of which is that all who follow the pope will land in the bottomless pit. And the book had its effect; it distressed Elizabeth's soul no end. To balance it, she began reading books that Antonio Filicchi secured for her from a priest in New York: Robert Manning's *England's Conversion* and a second work entitled *Reformation Compared*.

Back and forth she swayed, still attending services in her own denomination, yet becoming less and less comfortable. She went to Saint Paul's Chapel on Broadway for Sunday service and reported to Amabilia Filicchi:

> I got in a side pew which turned my face towards the Catholic Church in the next street, and found myself twenty times speaking to the Blessed Sacrament *there*, instead of looking at the naked altar where I was. [7]

Some time later, she wrote to Amabilia's husband, Antonio:

---

[6] John Henry Hobart, cited in Annabelle M. Melville, *Elizabeth Bayley Seton* (New York: Charles Scribner's Sons, 1951), 85–86.

[7] Elizabeth Seton to Amabilia Filicchi, cited in Dirvin, *Mrs. Seton*, 154.

After reading the life of St. Mary Magdalen, I thought: "Come my soul, let us turn from all these suggestions of one side or the other, and quietly resolve to go to that church which has at least the multitude of the wise and good on its side"; and began to consider the first step I must take. The first step—is it not to declare I believe all that is taught by the Council of Trent? [8]

One event that may have finalized her decision to convert was an action taken by the Anglican Church. In 1783 the church took as its official name the Protestant Episcopal Church. At the new church's first general convention, held in Philadelphia in 1789, the Anglican Book of Common Prayer was revised. Among the significant revisions was this: the former Book of Common prayer had stated that at communion "the Body and Blood of Christ . . . are verily and indeed taken and received by the faithful in the Lord's Supper." After the revision it said the Body and Blood of Christ are "spiritually taken and received". [9]

The old wording explains Elizabeth's intense devotion to the Anglican sacrament and her eagerness to accept the uncompromising Roman Catholic belief in the Real Presence. To Amabilia Filicchi she wrote:

A day of days for me. . . . I have been where?—to the Church of St. Peter with the cross on the top instead of a weather-cock! . . . When I turned the corner of the street it is in— "Here, my God, I go," said I, "[my] *heart all to You*". [10]

Mrs. Seton was received into the Catholic Church by Father William O'Brien on March 14, 1805, at Saint Peter's Church on Barclay Street. She paid dearly for her action. Her

[8] Elizabeth Seton to Antonio Filicchi, cited in ibid., 155.
[9] Dirvin, *Mrs. Seton*, 163, footnote.
[10] Elizabeth Seton to Amabilia Filicchi, cited in ibid., 164.

former friends and fellow parishioners thought she was mad, and they developed a bitter opposition to her. Many of them tried to persuade parents to remove their children from a small boarding school she had opened for her own livelihood. Eventually, she left New York and with her children went to Baltimore, where she engaged in similar work.

The rest of her story is known worldwide. A group of like-minded women whom she had gathered around her became the core, the nucleus, of the Sisters of Charity. On Paca Street in Baltimore, one can still visit the chapel where Elizabeth Bayley Seton and the others professed their vows.

From Baltimore, Mother Seton and her community moved to the small hamlet of Emmitsburg, Maryland, not far from the Pennsylvania border. Today, one may visit here the tomb of this very American saint, enshrined in a beautiful basilica on the grounds, as well as the graves of two of her five children in an adjoining cemetery. In this quiet, peaceful corner of rural America, Catholic education in the United States had its beginnings. Here, too, was the start of five major divisions of the Sisters of Charity in the United States and Canada. All this exists because of one woman's thirst for the Real Presence of our Lord in the Blessed Sacrament.

At the time of her canonization in 1975, in his foreword to a biography of Mother Seton, Terence Cardinal Cooke summed up her legacy:

> In Elizabeth Ann Seton, we have a saint for our times.
>
> In Elizabeth Ann Seton, we have a woman of faith, for a time of doubt and uncertainty . . . a woman of love for a time of coldness and division . . . a woman of hope for a time of crisis and discouragement.
>
> Thanks be to God for this saintly daughter of New York, for this valiant woman of God's Church.[11]

---

[11] Terence Cardinal Cooke, cited in ibid., xiii.

THE OXFORD MOVEMENT

What was it? Who came into the Church as a result of it?

In his book *The Spirit of the Oxford Movement*, the Catholic convert historian Christopher Dawson captures well a religious and academic setting:

> Oxford was the sacred city of Anglicanism, into which nothing common or unclean could enter, where neither popery nor Dissent could gain a foothold . . . it was inefficient, cumbersome, out of date. But it was beautiful; more beautiful perhaps than any other place in an England which was still rich in beauty; and consequently it could still inspire loyalty and affection.[1]

The town being referred to is, of course, England's medieval university community, and the period of time with which we are concerned is the 1830s. By then, not only had Oxford been in existence for centuries, but the Protestant Reformation was nearly three hundred years old. In other words, by the 1830s the Anglican tradition had had a long and established history at this university and, indeed, throughout the country.

Such history had important components that accounted for the Church of England's makeup in the 1830s. Four decades earlier, the French Revolution, with all of its radicalism

---

[1] Christopher Dawson, *The Spirit of the Oxford Movement* (New York: Sheed and Ward, 1933), 86–87.

directed against Church and state, had produced a negative reaction in England. In a nation where the monarch was head of the Church, devotion to Church and king was the very test of patriotism. Any pulling away from this devotion, as had occurred in France, further intensified patriotism across the Channel.

In England, this loyalty was closely allied to an almost fanatical hatred of foreign "popery", that is, the Catholic Church. Also, by the 1830s, an old alliance between the monarchy and the Tory (Conservative) party had been renewed. The High Church party had gained great influence, it believed in a strong Church–state alliance, and many of its beliefs were being expressed by the finest political thinkers and writers of the day.

Finally, the decade in which the Oxford Movement was born saw an extraordinary flowering of the national genius. Much of the parochialism of earlier decades was gone; English intellectual life was flourishing and enabling the British to engage more effectively in international debate. It is within this historical context that the Oxford Movement can be discussed most effectively.

What was it?

The movement was an effort on the part of several Oxford theologians to examine the Church of England from within and from without. From within, they concentrated on her teaching authority; from without, her relationship with the state as it existed in the nineteenth century.

In the first instance, the validity of her teaching, the theologians proceeded in much the same way Catholic apologists would. Going back to the time of our Lord's commission to Peter, they traced an uninterrupted line of succession to the sixteenth century. The Reformation was their point of departure. They seemed to be saying the Catholic Church had become so corrupt that reforms were not only necessary but justified. The Reformers merely purified, rather than invalidating the apostolicity of the Church. The irony of this was that many who became Catholics as a result of the Oxford Movement, and in later years as well, did so because of their conviction that such an argument could not be substantiated.

Secondly, the movement addressed the relationship between Church and state, especially the idea of Erastianism, which held that the Church of England should be subordinate to the civil authority. The Church did operate in the temporal order, the Oxford theologians said, though its reality was spiritual. Hence, it had a life of its own and should not be described or categorized in human terms. This view was critical, not only of state dominance of the Church, but also of liberal versus conservative, Low Church versus High Church factions within Anglicanism.

The Oxford theologians who expressed such views did so in pamphlets, or tracts. Their movement quickly became known as Tractarianism. Among them, John Henry Newman is unquestionably the towering figure. Other leaders were John Keble, Hurrell Froude, and E. B. Pusey. Of these, Keble, Froude, and Pusey remained Anglicans despite their strong Roman leanings. But Newman was to become the best-known convert of the century.

Of all the leaders, John Keble was considered the least original or creative in thought, perhaps because his point of view was very little modified in the course of the movement. He was the stable, unchanging force that such a movement requires, and he was one of the last of the old Tory, High Church tradition.

Keble sacrificed a brilliant career at Oxford and the prospect of future advancement in order to act as a curate for his father, also an Anglican minister, in the Cotswolds. And, if his devotion to his father was strong, equally strong was his devotion to the principle of loyalty to Church and state. Obedience to lawful rulers was, he thought, as sacred and divinely commanded a duty as filial obedience to parents.

Keble very much molded Hurrell Froude; he oriented Froude's mind in a religious direction and inspired him with a consuming desire for moral perfection. Froude, in much of his writing, conceived the human mind as having the potential for a spiritual vision, a vision that could be realized only by a process of moral steps gradually shaping the soul into a harmony with the invisible realities of the world of faith.[2]

John Henry Newman, the third of this very influential group, once described himself as the "rhetorician" of the group, while Keble and Froude were the "philosophers". Nevertheless, it was because of Newman that the movement reached a real crisis. It was because of one of Newman's pamphlets, Tract 90, published in 1841, that the movement became controversial. He argued that the Thirty-nine Articles[3] were, in essence, Catholic teaching as it was understood in the early Church and as it was defined at the Council of Trent. For such views, Newman was forced to resign as a fellow (professor) at Oriel College, Oxford. Further, it was determined he should no longer preach in the university church of Saint Mary the Virgin.

With so much of its emphasis on authority, doctrine, philosophy, theology, and rhetoric, one could easily think that the Oxford Movement was simply academic. But these "Tractarians" also developed a spiritual vision. They looked at

[2] For extended treatment on Keble and Froude, see R. W. Church, *The Oxford Movement* (Chicago: University of Chicago Press, 1970), 23–50.

[3] The Thirty-nine Articles, written in 1563 during the reign of Queen Elizabeth, defined the Creed of the Anglican Church broadly and ambiguously enough that persons of all shades of belief could be easily accommodated.

an Anglican Church that had grown lethargic; they wanted to reinvigorate it and give it an independence, particularly a spiritual independence.

Professor Owen Chadwick, a distinguished scholar writing from an objective, though non-Catholic, perspective, considered that the Oxford Movement was not something that should be identified merely by its philosophical conclusions or its doctrinal propositions. Rather, it was more a movement of the heart than the head, primarily concerned with the law of prayer and only secondarily with the law of belief:

> [T]he Creed was the Creed . . . the truth; not a noise of words to evoke prayer. But it roused the mind to prayer, and only through prayer and life was it known to be truth.

In this same vein, Chadwick continued:

> Certainly the principal changes which it brought in English life were changes in the mode of worship, or in the understanding of sanctity, or in the consequent methods of religious practice; and the changes of theological or philosophical thinking were, by comparison, less far reaching.[4]

All of that is undoubtedly true. We, however, must see the Oxford Movement as a phenomenon that brought many converts to the Church of Rome, both Anglican clergy and laity, and even dissenters. This was true not only in England but in the United States as well.

Who were some of the famous converts who came to the Catholic Church as a result of the Oxford Movement?

1. William George Ward, the father of Wilfrid Ward and grandfather of Maisie Ward (who married the Catholic publisher Frank Sheed). William George Ward and his wife were

---

[4] Owen Chadwick, *The Mind of the Oxford Movement* (London: Adam and Charles Black, 1960), 11–12.

both received into the Catholic Church in 1845 (the same year as Newman). At the time, they were living at Oxford, where they were very much influenced by the Tractarians and their writings. Once in the fold, they wanted to move to the vicinity of some great Catholic college, and Cardinal Nicholas Wiseman, then archbishop of Westminster, suggested that they move near Saint Edmund's College at Old Hall Green, near Ware. That college was descended from the English College at Douai on the Continent, where Catholics had been educated since the reign of Queen Elizabeth I. William Ward was a poor man when he moved to Old Hall, but some time later he inherited a large family property on the Isle of Wight, which apparently improved the family fortune substantially. He was, as we can gather from his own comments, a large man physically: " 'I have the mind of an archangel,' he once said, 'in the body of a rhinoceros.' " [5]

And he was a man who had a sharp intellect. He moved from being an ardent disciple of Matthew Arnold to an equally ardent disciple of John Henry Newman. An early historian of the Oxford Movement describes Ward in this way:

> Few more powerful intellects passed through Oxford in his time, and he has justified his University reputation by his distinction since, both as a Roman Catholic theologian and professor, and as a profound metaphysical thinker, the equal antagonist on their own ground of J. Stuart Mill and Herbert Spencer.[6]

In 1878, William Ward became editor of the *Dublin Review*. He was fiercely loyal to Rome, and in the spectrum of thought in convert circles he was on the far right. He detested liberal-

[5] Maisie Ward, *The Wilfrid Wards and the Transition* (London: Sheed and Ward, 1934), 1:6.

[6] R. W. Church, op. cit., 163, cited in Ward, *Wilfrid Wards*, 1:6.

ism in religion, the view that objective truth was not obtainable. His granddaughter wrote of him: "He would have liked constant and daily guidance from Rome, 'a Papal Bull every morning with his [London] *Times* at breakfast.'"[7]

2. Ward had a close ally in another Oxford Movement convert, Henry Edward Manning. Manning came from a well-to-do family; he went to Oxford and, after becoming an Anglican minister, was assigned as a country curate. He rose quickly in the Church of England because of his administrative skill and speaking ability, and by 1840 he was archdeacon of Chichester.

Manning had married as a young man, but his wife died after only a few brief years. His book *The Unity of the Church* further confirmed his Anglican credentials and made him a public figure at a comparatively young age.[8] Like so many, his reading of the Oxford Tracts was decisive in his journey to Rome, though his initial difficulties seem to have been less theological than political. Manning could not abide with the subservience of the Church of England to the government. In fact, years later, long after his ordination to the priesthood and his rise to cardinal archbishop of Westminster, he became a staunch promoter of the doctrine of papal infallibility at the First Vatican Council. He considered this doctrine to be a sure way to curb the power of the civil government.

As head of the Catholic Church in England, Cardinal Manning dedicated himself to convert making, and one of his friends, Florence Nightingale, came very close to being

[7] Ward, op. cit., 1:8.

[8] Proof of his public persona is a well-publicized article he wrote in 1845, sharply critical of John Henry Newman's conversion. By contrast, some years later, when Manning became a Catholic, his old friend the liberal Prime Minister William Gladstone let it be known he took it as a personal affront.

received into the Church. Shane Leslie, a biographer of Manning, noted that Miss Nightingale told the cardinal such a conversion would not be a sacrifice: "In Germany . . . they know why they are Protestants. I never knew an Englishman who did, and if he inquires, he becomes a Catholic!" [9] For reasons of her own, however, she never took that significant step.

3. Frederick William Faber, yet another Oxford Movement convert, was born in 1814, the son of an Anglican minister in Yorkshire. He went to Oxford, listened to Newman preach in the university church, and quickly became a Newmanite. He entered the Anglican ministry and was assigned to a church in Elton. In 1844 he wrote to Newman:

> I seem to grow more Roman daily, and almost to write from out the bosom of the Roman Church instead of from where I am. I suppose I am not going on as I ought to do, for our system seems more and more to enervate me, and I sometimes get a glimpse of a state of mind which would view my position as a parish priest as that of a man telling a lie to people.[10]

Newman's conversion in 1845 made a tremendous impression on this very poetic, literary man. Once Faber made his own decision to convert, he told his good friend William Wordsworth. Wordsworth replied: "I do not say you are wrong; but England loses a poet." [11]

---

[9] Florence Nightingale, cited in Shane Leslie, *Henry Edward Manning, His Life and Labors* (Westport, Conn.: Greenwood, 1970), 111.

[10] Frederick William Faber to John Henry Newman, 1844, cited in Wilfrid Woolen, *Father Faber* (London: Catholic Truth Society, 1962), 8.

[11] William Wordsworth to Frederick William Faber, 1842, cited in Woolen, op. cit., 4.

That, of course, was not correct. As a priest, as an Oratorian, and as founder of London's famous Brompton Oratory, Faber became one of Catholic England's most beloved spiritual writers, producing such works as *All for Jesus*, *Growth in Holiness*, *The Creator and the Creature*, *The Foot of the Cross*, and *The Precious Blood* and writing such magnificent hymns as "Faith of Our Fathers".

Such were typical Oxford converts. The movement's life span was at least a dozen years. Later, several naturalist strains of thought, born in the nineteenth century, seemed to overtake the movement's spiritual vision. From the perspective of faith, however, it was a movement of enormous consequence, both in England and in the United States, where also it attracted many significant converts. Best remembered, though, is its most towering intellect, John Henry Newman.

3

JOHN HENRY NEWMAN

The Oxford Movement's most famous convert

From the time that I became a Catholic, . . . [I] have had no anxiety of heart whatever. I have been in perfect peace and contentment; I never have had one doubt . . . and my happiness on that score remains to this day without interruption.[1]

Words spoken with deep conviction by a man who knew he had made the right choice in life and who was the greatest intellectual force behind the Oxford Movement. In November 1879, a friend of his who was an Anglican clergyman wrote to him: "I wonder if any man, at least of our time, was ever so loved by England." [2]

Who, then, was this venerable citizen?

John Henry Newman was born February 21, 1801, in the City of London.[3] He was the eldest of six children, and his family members were practicing, if not devout, Anglicans. Regular church attendance and evening prayers in common were accepted practice, but beyond that the family does not

[1] John Henry Newman, *Apologia pro Vita Sua* (New York: W. W. Norton and Company, 1968), 184.

[2] Vincent Ferrer Blehl, S.J., "John Henry Newman: 1801–1890", in *John Henry Newman: A Study in Holiness* (London: The Guild of Our Lady of Ransom, 1991), 6.

[3] The home on old Broad Street stood on ground now occupied by the London Stock Exchange. A plaque at the visitors' entrance marks the exact spot.

appear to have been identified with either branch of the Church of England, High or Low.

From his earliest years, young Newman had a wonderful intellect. It is rare to find boys seven years of age proficient in music. It is rarer still to find boys of fifteen experiencing profound crises of faith. Nonetheless, at seven, he was an accomplished violinist, and more than one commentator has noted that the rhythm of his prose writing is traceable to his keen musical sense. As a student at Ealing, a private boarding school, his interest in theology reached such proportions that his doubts in matters of faith were those often reached much later in the thought processes of life, if indeed reached at all. One of his professors suggested specific readings to calm his disturbed mind, and from those he had a deep conversion experience. He took a private vow of celibacy, began taking frequent communion in the Anglican Church, prayed regularly, and meditated often on Scripture. This formed the pattern for a very holy life, so holy, in fact, that most people would be quite surprised to discover his lifelong inner struggles with such things as pride, self-esteem, and the continuous control of his temper.

At the age of twenty-one, Newman's scholarly and religious lives converged. He was appointed a Fellow (professor) at Oriel College, Oxford, and he became a minister in the Church of England. He displayed a pastoral zeal in his first assignment as curate of Saint Clement's, Oxford, and it was not long before he was named vicar of the university church of Saint Mary the Virgin. Years later, he reminisced about that appointment: "It was to me like the feeling of spring weather after winter; and if I may so speak, I came out of my shell." [4]

In 1833, he wrote his first major book, *The Arians of the*

[4] Blehl, loc. cit., 9.

Fourth Century. A dozen years later (the same year he became a Catholic), he wrote his famous *Essay on the Development of Christian Doctrine*. In the intervening years, his scholarly output was impressive.[5] Much of this scholarship coincided with his love of, and appreciation for, the Fathers of the Church. He chose to single out at least two: "The broad philosophy of Clement and Origen carried me away. Some portions of their teaching came like music to my inward ear." [6]

God had a specific plan for John Henry Newman, one that would unfold with each passing year. This was evident when, on a trip to Sicily, he became seriously ill but quickly recovered. His willingness to accept completely whatsoever God chose was expressed in a hymn he composed, a hymn that would be sung often in Anglican churches and is today a commonly known prayer:

> Lead, kindly Light, amid the encircling gloom,
> Lead Thou me on!
> The night is dark, and I am far from home—
> Lead Thou me on!
> Keep Thou my feet; I do not ask to see
> The distant scene,—one step enough for me.[7]

Most important to his development was his leadership of the Oxford Movement in the 1830s. Newman viewed the movement as a wonderful opportunity for the spiritual renewal of Anglican clergy and laity, and he continually developed this theme in the sermons he preached in the university church of Saint Mary the Virgin and in the parish church of

---

[5] It consisted of tracts, book-length treatises, lectures, articles, book reviews, collections of sermons, editions of the works of the Fathers, and republished Anglican spiritual works. See Blehl, loc. cit., 11.

[6] Ibid., 10.

[7] Wilfrid Ward, *The Life of John Henry Cardinal Newman* (London: Longmans, Green, 1921), 1:55.

Littlemore, a small village close to Oxford, where he had assumed the duties of vicar. These masterpieces of spiritual literature later were collected and published as his *Parochial and Plain Sermons*.

In addition to spiritual renewal, the movement had three other points of great significance for Newman:

1. A battle against liberalism in religion, a liberalism that he straightaway defined:

> That truth and falsehood in religion are but matter of opinion; that one doctrine is as good as another; that the Governor of the world does not intend that we should gain the truth; that there is no truth; that we are not more acceptable to God by believing this than by believing that; that no one is answerable for his opinions; that they are a matter of necessity or accident; that it is enough if we sincerely hold what we profess; that our merit lies in seeking not in possessing; that it is a duty to follow what seems to us true, without a fear lest it should not be true; that it may be a gain to succeed, and can be no harm to fail; that we may take up and lay down opinions at pleasure; that belief belongs to the mere intellect, not to the heart also; that we may safely trust to ourselves in matters of Faith, and need no other guide.[8]

2. An opportunity to assert there was such a thing as religious teaching, and it was based in doctrine: "That there was a visible Church, with sacraments and rites which are the channels of invisible grace." [9]

3. A protest against what Newman thought at the time were the corruptions of Rome.[10]

---

[8] John Henry Newman, cited in Ian Ker, *John Henry Newman: A Biography* (Oxford: Oxford University Press, 1988), 312.

[9] Blehl, loc. cit., 11.

[10] For a detailed treatment of Newman's early doubts about the Roman Church, see Ker, op. cit., 62–71, 158–212.

The corruptions of the Church of Rome he would ultimately be able to reconcile. His first two points of far-reaching consequence had their foundation in his study of the Church Fathers. They led him to an even stronger reflection: "The great truth that the Anglican Church is in a state of schism had possession of my mind." [11]

By 1839, however, he could not yet profess the belief that the fullness of faith was found in Rome. Still, if God's grace were given him, he would try "not to be unfaithful to the light given him". [12]

Ultimately, against all his inclinations, Newman was forced to admit that his own studies of the Church Fathers were undermining his previous conclusions, especially the validity of Anglican claims to truth.

He was forced to resign the rectorship of the university church, as well as his fellowship at Oriel College. He then retired to his flock at Littlemore, tended to them, and lived at least a semi-monastic life.

There followed six more years of agonizing over his religious position, which he described some twenty years later when he wrote his *Apologia pro Vita Sua*, an explanation of his life or, as one of his biographers has described it, an intellectual autobiography. [13] What puzzled him most were points of Catholic doctrine that could not be found specifically in Scripture or in the Fathers. He continued his studies and consulted with Charles Russell, president of Maynooth College in Ireland.

The outcome of these anguished years was the publication in 1845 of his *Essay on the Development of Christian Doctrine*. This was his pre-conversion work, and in it he argued that the

[11] Blehl, loc. cit., 13.
[12] Ibid., 13.
[13] Ker, op. cit., 548.

original deposit of faith, though complete, was not always fully elaborated in the early Church and that the full unfolding of doctrines often required the challenge of historical crises. When studied in this way, what might appear as innovations could be explained, since the Church of any age rests on the same dogmatic foundations.

Nevertheless, Newman had a firm sense of duty and strong emotional ties to Oxford. These held him back from 1841 to 1845. Many of his close friends preceded him into the Church, until in 1845 he finally "went over to Rome", causing a tremendous sensation in British life.

In the fall of 1845 he preached his final sermon as an Anglican minister, "The Parting of Friends". Afterward, he retired to his residence, "The College", as it was called, directly across from the Anglican church in Littlemore. Like Newman Centers in many parts of the world, it is staffed today by religious women of the International Community of the Work, a community founded some decades ago by Mother Julia Verhaeghe in Belgium. Newman thought well of this venerable building: "[T]here it is that I have both been taught my way, and received an answer to my prayers." [14]

The answer to his prayers came on October 9 when Father (now Blessed) Dominic Barberi, of the Passionist Congregation, received him into the Catholic Church. In a letter to Henry Wilberforce, Newman tells the story himself:

Father Dominic, the Passionist, is passing this way, on his way from Aston in Staffordshire to Belgium, where a chapter of his Order is to be held at this time. He is to come to Littlemore for the night as a guest of one of us whom he has admitted at Aston. He does not know of my intentions, but I shall ask of

[14] J. H. Newman to W. J. Copeland, October 3, 1848, cited in "The College" (Littlemore: Ambrose Cottage), 1.

him admission into the One true fold of the Redeemer. I shall keep this back till after it is all over. . . .

I was not sorry to accept this matter of time at an inconvenience, to submit myself to what seemed an eternal call. Also, I suppose the departure of others has had something to do with it. . . .

Father Dominic has had his thoughts turned to England from a youth, in a distinct and remarkable way. He has had little or nothing to do with conversions, but goes on missions and retreats among his own people. . . . He is a simple, quaint man, an Italian; but a very sharp clever man too in his way. It is an accident his coming here and I had no thoughts of applying to him till quite lately, nor should I suppose, but for this accident.[15]

Newman tells much of this in his work *Loss and Gain*. The book follows a fictitious character named Charles Redding, an Oxford undergraduate on his path to Rome, and his reception into the Church by one Father Albert, a Passionist. Newman must have been writing about himself when he described the new convert as "so happy in the present, that he has no thoughts either for the past or for the future".[16] This book was widely read by the British public when it appeared in 1848, and there can be little doubt it brought many who were wavering to follow his example.

Newman's conversion was very much an intellectual one. He came to the Church by a thought process.

I am a Catholic by virtue of my believing in God; and if I am asked why I believe in a God, I answer that it is because I believe in myself, for I feel it impossible to believe in my own

[15] J. H. Newman to Henry Wilberforce, October 7, 1845, cited in Ward, op. cit., 1:92–93.
[16] John Henry Newman, *Loss and Gain* (London: Burns and Oates, 1962), 246.

existence . . . without believing also in the existence of Him,
who lives as a . . . Being in my conscience.[17]

He developed his own belief as only an intellectual could.

People say that the doctrine of Transubstantiation is difficult
to believe; I did not believe the doctrine till I was a Catholic.
I had no difficulty in believing it, as soon as I believed that the
Catholic Roman Church was the oracle of God, and that she
had declared this doctrine to be part of the original revelation.
It is difficult, impossible, to imagine, I grant;—but how is it
difficult to believe?[18]

In other words, for Newman, the question was not if it was
possible to believe honestly in particular Catholic doctrines,
but whether the entire Catholic system as such is honest or
dishonest.

Newman, like so many others, gave up a great deal and
endured much criticism for becoming a Catholic. He compared his leaving Littlemore to a voyage one would take on
the open sea, fraught with uncertainties. This voyage, by his
own admission, was made so much easier through his faith in
our Lord's Real Presence in the Blessed Sacrament.

After his conversion, Newman and a number of his associates lived together, much as he had lived a communitarian life
at Littlemore. He chose to call this new residence Maryvale.
Within two years of his reception into the Church, he was
ordained to the Catholic priesthood at the Collegio Propa-
ganda Fidei, close by the Spanish Steps in Rome. Back in his
native land he joined the Congregation of the Oratory, more
commonly called Oratorians, founded around three centuries
earlier by Saint Philip Neri. Newman had received a papal

---

[17] John Henry Newman, cited in Ker, op. cit., 549.
[18] Newman, *Apologia*, 184–85.

brief (directive) while in Rome to set up an Oratory in Birmingham.

Father Newman, great intellect and writer that he was, also became the Oratorian priest performing the most mundane of duties in the Oratory, dispensing Christ's sacraments to the faithful, carrying out parochial ministrations familiar to priests, and doing all with great joy.

He made magnificent contributions to his new Faith: At the invitation of the Irish hierarchy, he crossed the channel to establish the Catholic University of Ireland in Dublin. From this experience came much of his material for *The Idea of a University*. In his *Letter to Pusey*, he defended devotion to our Lady and presented a balanced Catholic view. When William Gladstone attacked the civic loyalty of English Catholics (after the definition of papal infallibility), Newman replied with his *Letter to the Duke of Norfolk*, in which he showed the truly moderate and unalarming nature of the doctrine of infallibility.

There were few, if any, persons of significance in England who did not give Newman their respect, and in 1879, when Pope Leo XIII gave him the cardinal's hat, the civic receptions and public response clearly showed a nation's admiration.

It did not change him. Newman the cardinal continued as Newman the Oratorian until his death in 1890. He lived unassumingly in the Birmingham community he had begun with his fellow priests. Upon his death the *Birmingham Daily Post* commented significantly: "[H]is character was the chief instrument in destroying the bigoted hatred of Roman Catholicism which had almost become an English tradition." [19]

And for us—what are we to take from the life of this convert cardinal? Perhaps John Paul II said it best on his 1982

[19] Blehl, loc. cit., 28.

visit to England: "[I]mitate his humility and his obedience to God; pray for a wisdom like his, a wisdom that can come from God alone." [20]

---

[20] *Birmingham Daily Post*, undated, cited in Blehl, loc. cit., 28.

4

ROSE HAWTHORNE LATHROP

Foundress of the Hawthorne Dominicans

The most important news I have to tell you (if you have not already heard it), is that we have another daughter, now about two months old. She is a very bright and healthy child, and neither more or less handsome than babies generally are. I think I feel more interest in her than I did in the other children at the same age, from the consideration that she is to be the daughter of my age—the comfort (at least, so it is to be hoped) of my declining years.[1]

This passage was written from Lenox, Massachusetts, in 1851, by the famous American author Nathaniel Hawthorne. He was informing a friend of the birth of his daughter Rose Hawthorne on May 20 of that year. Hers was to be a life far different from the tradition into which she was born.

Rose was the youngest of three children born to Hawthorne and his wife, Sophia Peabody. Sophia was the daughter of a schoolteacher, Elizabeth Palmer Peabody. Her mother has been described as "intelligent and socially conscious . . . , extraordinarily well-read, not only in the classics

---

[1] This letter, undated and sent to "an old friend", is cited in Boniface Hanley, O.F.M., "The More Things Change, the More They Are the Same", *The Anthonian* (Patterson, N.J.: Saint Anthony's Guild, 1985), 59:3.

of literature known in English nineteenth century culture, but in the emerging new American literature".[2]

In their early years, the Peabody sisters, Mary, Elizabeth, and Sophia, were exposed to the exceptional literary culture of New England. Elizabeth served for a time as secretary to the famous Unitarian preacher William Ellery Channing. His sermons were classics of American religious literature, protesting as they did much of the fatalism found in Calvinistic theology.

Sophia carefully read the works of Ralph Waldo Emerson, and she was much taken with them. She was equally taken with a young author, Nathaniel Hawthorne, who had written a book called *Twice-Told Tales*, and who, in the early 1840s, came to visit the Peabody home. He had recently experienced Brook Farm, an experiment in communal living, and decided it was not to be his future. No doubt wishing to settle down and establish a stable life and career, he and Sophia Peabody were married in July 1842.

Their first home was the old manse in Concord, Massachusetts. To this day, it remains a popular tourist attraction because of the many famous names who occupied it. From Concord, the family moved to Salem, site of the famous colonial witchcraft trials, and finally to Lenox, where their youngest daughter, Rose, was born in 1851. Herman Melville, another New England author, was their neighbor in Lenox, and it was there Hawthorne began writing *The House of the Seven Gables*. The family returned, finally, to Concord, where they purchased the home of Bronson Alcott and named it Wayside.

The election of Franklin Pierce as president of the United States in 1852 was to change the Hawthornes' lives consider-

[2] Diana Culbertson, O.P. ed., *Rose Hawthorne Lathrop: Selected Writings* (New York: Paulist Press, 1993), 3.

ably. Pierce was a friend of Nathaniel Hawthorne's, and after his election Pierce appointed Hawthorne American consul in Liverpool, England. The Hawthornes remained there for nearly six years, moving to Italy in 1858. During these years in Europe, young Rose's education was provided by tutors, governesses, and, most often, her parents. Nathaniel and Sophia Hawthorne had a great love for their three children, Julian, Una, and Rose, and they were unsparing in the amount of time they spent with them and the training they gave them.

It would be difficult for anyone to experience the Italian ambiance without encountering things Catholic. The Hawthornes were no exception. Nathaniel wrote of his experiences in the Dominican church of Santa Maria Novella in Florence, the same church, coincidentally, where young Rose, a future Dominican sister, was particularly attracted to a statue of the seventeenth-century Dominican tertiary Saint Rose of Lima. The chapter house of Santa Maria Novella, with its sacramental life, would remind any Catholic of a bustling parish church. Hawthorne noted:

> The cool dusky refreshment of these holy places, affording such a refuge from the hot noon of the streets and piazzas, probably suggests devotional ideas to the people, and it may be, when they are praying, they feel a breath of Paradise fanning them. If we could only see any good effects in their daily life, we might deem it an excellent thing to be able to find incense and a prayer always ascending, to which every individual may join his own. I really wonder that Catholics are not better men and women.[3]

It is hard to say if this early exposure to things Catholic had any great effect on Rose Hawthorne. It certainly had little on

---

[3] Nathaniel Hawthorne, cited in Culbertson, op. cit., 8.

her sister Una. She wrote of "the idolatrous mummeries of the Catholic Church" and the "miserable Romish religion".[4]

The Hawthornes returned in 1860 to Wayside, their home in Concord. Nathaniel was to live only four more years; his death came in 1864, a result of an illness that had weakened him gradually since the family's return from the Continent.

Although he had been a literary success, Nathaniel Hawthorne apparently did not leave his widow financially stable. Because of her circumstances, Sophia moved her family to Dresden, Germany, where she enrolled Rose in a private school. It was not a particularly happy experience for the young woman, but this must have been forgotten rather quickly when she met her future husband, George Parsons Lathrop, a young man who also happened to be living in Dresden. They fell in love and were married seven months later at Saint Luke's Anglican church in the Chelsea section of London. Returning to America, George joined the staff of the *Atlantic Monthly*, then edited by William Dean Howells.

Their marriage was not a very happy one. They had one little boy, who died very young, devastating both of them. George turned to alcohol, and alcoholism was to plague him in some fashion or other for the remainder of his life. Rose began to write short stories for such publications as *Harper's*, the *American*, and the *Ladies' Home Journal*.

In 1891 this well-known, influential couple shocked the literary establishment, Rose's native New England, their respective families, and, one would think, many others besides with the announcement that they were both being received into the Roman Catholic Church. Neither of them described in detail their inner feelings; nonetheless, some clues about their conversion may be discovered from their religious backgrounds.

---

[4] Una Hawthorne, cited in Culbertson, op. cit., 9.

There is no evidence that Rose and George Lathrop had actively practiced Christianity. When they became Catholics, one press account noted they had been agnostics prior to their conversion. George Lathrop felt the need to respond. He stated he had never been an unbeliever and had, in fact, been baptized in the Episcopalian church. His wife, Rose, had been raised a Unitarian by parents who were "full of reverence for Christ, little differing in devoutness from that paid to him as the Son of God, one with the Trinity".[5]

Rose's Unitarianism had grown out of the Transcendental Movement. Transcendentalism combined elements of Romanticism with belief in supernatural light. It was individualistic and democratic in outlook. It did not have much dogmatic content. Unitarianism had even less. Rose had a faith-filled mother, and this influence, far more than any intellectual probing, contributed to her spiritual development.

Opinions vary on who was most influential in the Lathrops' conversion. Some historians think the Catholic poet, journalist, and editor John Boyle O'Reilly, a friend of George Lathrop's, may have been the first to speak to him about Catholicism. An even stronger influence, say others, was that of Alfred and Adelaide Huntington Chappel, converts with whom the Lathrops had become close. In any event, it appears George took the first step in the spiritual search, and, when both were ready, they began to prepare themselves by reading such works as Cardinal Gibbons' *Faith of Our Fathers*, Monsignor Capel's *The Faith of Catholics*, and Cardinal Nicholas Wiseman's *Lectures on Doctrines of the Church*. Nearly twenty years after they had been married in London, the Lathrops were received in full communion with the Church in New York City, at the Church of Saint

---

[5] George Lathrop, cited in Culbertson, op. cit., 24.

Paul the Apostle, on the Feast of Saint Joseph, March 19, 1891.[6]

In a letter to the editor of the *Boston Pilot*, George Lathrop described his intellectual journey to Catholicism. He did not mention his wife's journey to the Faith. He may have thought he was speaking for her, or he may have felt her reasons were privately her own.

> No one ever suggested my becoming a Catholic, or tried to persuade me; although a number of my friends were Catholics. . . . Notwithstanding that my education had surrounded me with prejudice, my mind was convinced as to the truth, the validity and supremacy of the Roman Catholic Church, by the clear and comprehensive reasoning upon which it is based. And while the reasoning of other religious organizations continually shifts and wavers, leaving their adherents— as we now see almost every day—to fall into rationalism and agnostic denial, the reasoning of the Church, I found, led directly into sublime and inspiring faith. This union of solid reasoning and luminous faith I cannot discover elsewhere.[7]

And to that, Lathrop offered a surprising comment on the consolations given him by the Catholic doctrine of the communion of saints:

> [T]he present active and incessant spirituality of the church does not stop short with this life or end in that pagan acceptance of death as an impassable barrier, which one meets with in Protestant denominations. It links together the religious souls of all periods, whether now on earth, or in the world beyond.[8]

---

[6] For more detail see Culbertson, op. cit., 31–32.

[7] George Lathrop to John Jeffrey Roche, March 24, 1891, cited in Culbertson, op. cit., 32–33. See also Hanley, op. cit., 11–12.

[8] Lathrop to Roche, cited in Culbertson, op. cit., 33.

Needless to say, not all the press coverage of Mr. and Mrs. Lathrop was favorable. One of the strong anti-Catholic arguments directed against them was that much Catholic belief was pious superstition that defied rational thought and made one who professed it appear childlike. Further, it was said that the Church calls for a blind obedience to its teachings, and those who submit to them can only be considered curious spectacles.[9]

Citing specific sources on the relationship between the Church's Faith and scientific thought, Lathrop responded: "Mr. Edison . . . has said that we do not yet know what electricity is. Does he therefore doubt its existence, or its immense importance? Or do any of us doubt it? Not at all!" [10]

He went further in trying to answer the charge of blind obedience to papal teaching:

> We Americans all bow to decrees of the [United States] Supreme Court and submit to proclamations by the President, even when those decrees and proclamations run counter to our individual wishes or opinions. But no one is so fatuous as to argue that, because we do this, we are the slaves of "unreasoning obedience." [11]

The new converts, Rose and George Lathrop, were to throw themselves into the service of the Church. Together they wrote a book entitled *A Story of Courage: A History of the Georgetown Visitation Convent*. In addition, they gave themselves to the Catholic Summer School Movement, then headquartered in New London, Connecticut. It was an attempt to

---

[9] The accusation was made by the *New York Independent*, a staunchly anti-Catholic publication. For more detail on the paper's comments and Lathrop's reply, see Culbertson, op. cit., 34.

[10] George Lathrop, cited in Culbertson, op. cit., 34.

[11] Ibid.

provide culture and education to those who participated, and it was based heavily on the Chautauqua Assembly begun by American Methodists.[12]

One biographer has captured the essence of Rose's spirituality as it began to develop in those years:

> Eucharistic devotion emerged most powerfully during the years that Rose was learning about Catholicism, and especially during the first decades of the twentieth century when she was entering more and more deeply into the life of the church. . . . Rose's devotion to the eucharist, which had clearly been urged upon her from the beginning, was never to diminish. All things distinctively Catholic she embraced without hesitation, and gradually that most distinctive life of all began to attract her: the visible presence of women consecrated publicly to the service of the Church.[13]

As noted, alcoholism afflicted George Lathrop much of his adult life. He became increasingly difficult to live with; the couple separated and remained apart until George's death. One of the bright spots in Rose's life, however, was her close friendship with a young Jewish girl named Emma Lazarus. Emma's name may not be familiar to all, but the thoughts she expressed are surely known, for they are her words that appear on the base of the Statue of Liberty:

> . . . "Give me your tired, your poor,
> Your huddled masses yearning to breathe free,
>   The wretched refuse of your teeming shore.
> Send these, the homeless, tempest-tost to me,
>   I lift my lamp beside the golden door!"[14]

Emma labored for Russia's persecuted Jews, and she was

[12] Culbertson, op. cit., 36.
[13] Ibid., 44.
[14] Hanley, op. cit., 11.

the first to interest Rose in the plight of the suffering. Emma's death from cancer increased Rose's concern for those afflicted with this disease, and when Rose discovered that New York City hospitals would not keep those suffering from incurable cancer and that their only recourse was to go to Roosevelt (Welfare) Island, she knew she had found her life's work.

After the death of her husband in 1898, Rose expressed a desire to adopt some style of religious life and to wear some distinctive garb. Because of the influence of a Dominican priest from Saint Vincent Ferrer's in Manhattan, Rose and a number of like-minded women professed their vows as Dominican sisters, after which she was known as Sister Mary Alphonsa. The sisters began Saint Rose's Home, on Water Street in Manhattan; later they moved the facility to Cherry Street.

A community of French Dominicans who were returning to France owned a property in Westchester County. Sister Alphonsa and Sister Rose Huber, who would one day succeed her, "took a Harlem River Division train of the New York Central Railroad, got off at the present site of Hawthorne, New York, and were led to a large frame house high on a hill".[15]

The house, of course, was to become Rosary Hill Home, the first free cancer clinic in the United States. The sisters have since become known as Hawthorne Dominicans for the Care of Incurable Cancer. In each of their facilities, Sister Alphonsa insisted on certain fixed principles. Do not express any repulsion at the sight of cancer; do not allow any patient to be used as an object for medical research; and do not take money from a patient's family or previous employer, on the theory that very soon only patients coming from families able to pay would be admitted.[16]

[15] Ibid., 23.
[16] Ibid., 21–23.

Samuel Clemens (Mark Twain), raised with a decided bias against Catholicism, was nonetheless one of Sister Alphonsa's earliest and steadiest benefactors. Over the years, countless others have imitated his generosity. Because of the vision of one convert, the poor, the sick, and the dying—all of whom represent Christ—receive a care that is hard to surpass. How blest those poor are that Rose Hawthorne Lathrop found the Catholic Faith.

5

IGNATIUS SPENCER

An English Passionist convert

If you are ever in Saint Peter's in Rome, look directly at the papal altar and the great columns of Bernini, then fix your gaze above the columns to the right: there you will see a statue of Saint Paul of the Cross. This saint, in the second half of the eighteenth century, began a religious community known as the Congregation of the Passion or, more popularly, the Passionists. The members of this order were to be devoted to preaching and to spreading devotion to the Passion of Christ. As a preaching order, they spread quickly to many countries of the world. In the course of the years, the Passionists have produced several converts whose lives were remarkable: one of these was an Englishman, George Spencer.

Before the American Revolution began, the Passionists were given charge of the monastery and church of Saints John and Paul on the Coelian Hill in Rome. It is a marvelous structure, built over the tombs of two brothers, John and Paul, early Christian martyrs in the city of Rome. It was, and remains, world headquarters for the Passionist community. Some decades ago, the great English travel writer H. V. Morton decided to pay these Passionists a visit. On his arrival he was greeted by one Father Alfred, an English Passionist from Lancashire. The priest led Mr. Morton around and, as Morton relates in his book *A Traveler in Rome*, they came to "a long corridor ... lined with the portraits of distinguished Passionists".

> Father Alfred paused in front of one: "Does he remind you of anyone?" he asked. "Yes," I replied. "Father Winston Churchill!" "Absolutely correct," said Father Alfred, "he is Father Ignatius Spencer, a Passionist, and a great uncle of Winston Churchill." [1]

The man to whom Father Alfred referred was known in the world as George Spencer. At the time of his birth in 1799, his father, George John, second Earl Spencer, was serving as first lord of the admiralty. Hence his son, the youngest of the Spencers' seven children, was born in Admiralty House in London. Not only his father's government position—but also the fact that his mother sat for Sir Joshua Reynolds, the most famous of early nineteenth-century portrait painters—indicates the level of society to which young George belonged.

Althrop, the Spencer ancestral estate, some distance from London, was home to George from the time he was one year old. His portrait hangs there with the rest of the Spencers, and apparently younger generations of the family considered him a bit curious. A story is told of a judge being given a tour of the portrait hall and, upon arriving at George's likeness, being informed he was one member of the family not spoken of a great deal, because he became a papist, worse yet, a priest. While this story may or may not have foundation, George Spencer and his six siblings remained very close, even after his conversion to the Church of Rome. His sister Lady Sarah Lyttelton was a lady-in-waiting to Queen Victoria. As a Catholic priest and a Passionist, her brother once asked if it would be acceptable to visit her in Buckingham Palace while

[1] H. V. Morton, *A Traveler in Rome* (New York: Dodd Mead and Co., 1957), 216.

wearing his religious habit. He probably would have done so, since he was known to visit Ten Downing Street, the prime minister's residence, attired thus. But Lady Sarah wrote back to her brother, begging him to consider the consequences his action might have, and visits with his sister were confined to her home.

It was at Althrop, when he was six years of age, that someone first spoke to George about spiritual things. A Swiss governess, obviously a devout woman, was fond of telling him about eternal life. Years later, he wrote: "Till then, I believe, I had not the least apprehension of the existence of anything beyond the sensible world around me." [2]

This episode could have sparked an interest in religion that began to blossom while he was a student at Eton, that famous educational institution so close to Windsor Castle. One of his teachers recommended he read John Bunyan's *Pilgrim's Progress*, and the work had enormous influence on him. It developed an evangelical piety that would last a lifetime. This piety, or what one writer has called seriousness, expressed itself in his prayer life and the intense disciplines of fasting and penance he would impose upon himself. Also at Eton, his scholarship began to develop, making his acceptance to Cambridge quite easy. He entered the university in 1817, and, before he graduated, had decided to take orders in the Church of England. Prior to that, however, his parents felt he should experience the Continent, and by so doing, he had his first real taste of Catholic culture. He found it to be "priests, processions, incense and mummery".[3]

While he enjoyed his sojourn, he was uncomfortable with the Catholic Church as he found it. He later wrote:

[2] Jerome Vereb, C.P., "Ignatius Spencer, Passionist: Apostle of Christian Unity" (Bolton: Coop Hunt and Co., n.d.), 3.

[3] Ibid., 4.

> I never had much pains taken with me to set me against the
> Catholic religion, but though I knew nothing of what it was,
> I rested in the conviction that it was full of superstition and in
> fact, as good as no religion at all.[4]

Looking back years later on that trip, he wrote: "It is remarkable how easily one's mind takes in and rests contented in the
belief of false and prejudicial representations of things." [5]

By 1824 George Spencer was a minister of the Church of
England, at a parish in Brington, near Northampton. It is
interesting to read in the life of converts how many have
suffered doubts of faith and, in their groping for answers, have
embraced the Catholic position. For Newman, these doubts
began at the age of fifteen and would not be fully resolved for
nearly thirty years. In Father Spencer's case, they came shortly
after taking Anglican orders and were resolved in a much
shorter time. As an Anglican, Spencer had been teaching
doctrines held by the Church of England that he could not
verify by a reading of Scripture. He could not yet appreciate
the fact that his ecclesial body lacked an official Magisterium
to interpret Scripture, as well as a tradition that is equally a
channel of God's revelation. Also, Spencer was torn with an
inner struggle. The evangelical piety, so much a part of his
makeup since student days, was seeking expression in a more
contemplative form of life. The busy parochial ministrations
of an Anglican vicar wreaked havoc with his emotions and
caused him to experience significant doubts.

Spencer met two Catholic priests—Father William Foley,
an Irishman working in the Brington area, and Dr. John
Fletcher, a noted apologist from the Douai seminary on the
Continent who was then serving as chaplain in the home of
Dowager Countess Throckmorton. Both these priests gave

[4] Ibid.
[5] Ibid., 5.

him support, strong encouragement, and friendship, but it was his friendship with Ambrose DeLisle, seventeen years old, that was the catalyst bringing him to the Catholic Church. DeLisle was a brilliant debater, especially with men decades older. After one of these debates, the two men struck up a lifelong friendship. DeLisle later married and spent his life trying to build up Catholicism in England, even bringing French Trappists to his land, where he established the first contemplative monastery in England since the Reformation.

In January 1830, George Spencer resigned his parish in Brington, and by the end of the month he had become a Catholic. Shortly thereafter he went to Rome to study for the priesthood, and, after only a year and a half, he was ordained on May 28, 1832, the feast of Saint Augustine of Canterbury, the great missionary sent to the English people centuries before by Pope Gregory the Great. In Rome, George Spencer met two men who were to influence his future significantly: Nicholas Wiseman, a future archbishop of Westminster, his rector at the venerable English College, and Passionist Father Dominic Barberi.

On his return to England, Father Spencer was appointed curate at the parish of Walsall, which covered a very large geographic area. He worked especially hard at making converts, and he opened three schools where the rudiments of the Faith were taught, not only to children, but to adults who had either never sufficiently learned them or who wanted to refresh themselves. Seven years of this parochial work were followed by another seven as spiritual director to seminarians at Oscott College.

George Spencer in one way anticipated the ecumenical movement: he saw the need for unity among Christian peoples, and, in May 1839, in a sermon he preached in Saint Chad's cathedral, Manchester, he explained his thoughts on the subject. The title of that sermon was "The Great Importance of Reunion between the Catholics and the Protestants of England, and the Method Effecting It".

As a former Anglican, he was in a unique position to remind Catholics in the congregation that non-Catholics were not evil people. Hostility on either side was an inexcusable thing and must be fought against. There were so many areas for mutual cooperation. Truth must always be the ultimate goal, but truth was never to be sacrificed in the interest of unity. As if to unburden his soul to each denomination, he said, first to Protestants:

> I believe you to be in error, and . . . I most ardently desire to lead you to believe as I do. However, Catholics can, and must, learn of their own misconduct from Protestants who should not hesitate to point out criticisms in charity so that Catholics might be worthy of union and that both groups might grow in holiness.[6]

Spencer called his crusade "Unity in the Truth", and he traveled throughout England asking Catholics and non-Catholics, each in their own way, to pray for this intention. He even went, in priestly garb, into the parlors of the prime minister asking him to pray for the same intention. In the 1840s he began the Association of Prayers and Good Works for the Conversion of Those Separated from the Holy Catholic Church, an association granted special papal blessings and indulgences to its members.

In his ongoing quest for holiness, George Spencer closely followed Saint Ignatius' *Spiritual Exercises*, in the hope that God's will would be made manifest in his life. It was. He felt the call to be a Passionist and contacted his old friend Dominic

[6] Ibid., 15.

Barberi, who had recently received Newman into the Church. After a private retreat, he presented himself to Father Dominic, and, in January 1847, he received the Passionist habit, taking the name Ignatius of Saint Paul. Father Jerome Vereb, in his essay "Ignatius Spencer, Passionist: Apostle of Christian Unity", continues the story:

> He was already a zealous apostle but now he learned to channel that zeal after the method of St. Paul of the Cross. He identified himself completely with the poor. There was no guaranteed income from the Spencer estate, only his vow of poverty. He followed the Passionist rule with its rigorous observance and above all, he preached the message of Jesus' Passion and Death in England and Ireland. On August 27, 1849, Dominic died while on his way to preach a mission and Ignatius found himself the superior of the Passionists in England, after little more than a year of professed life.[7]

Father Ignatius did much to organize and oversee the establishment of the English Province of Passionists. In addition, he gave a great deal of help to Elizabeth Prout, a convert from Shropshire who founded the Sisters of the Cross and Passion and who in religion was known as Mother Mary Joseph Prout.

This very holy man, Ignatius, was in constant demand as a Passionist missionary throughout England and Ireland. He died in 1864 and is buried at Saint Anne's Retreat, Sutton, Lancashire, next to Blessed Dominic Barberi and Mother Mary Joseph. A great convert, a great priest, a great missionary, a great Passionist, a great Englishman.

---

[7] Ibid., 18.

6

ORESTES BROWNSON AND ISAAC HECKER

Two American Transcendentalists

Many of the Church's converts have come to her after a variety of religious experiences. At least two were conspicuous for their early involvement in the Transcendental Movement. In looking more closely at their lives, we must investigate a bit more this movement that played such a significant role in nineteenth-century American religious thought.

In essence, Transcendentalism was based on the idea that all principles of reality are to be discovered by the processes of thought, that is, with an emphasis on the intuitive and the spiritual above the empirical. It was a strain of thought popularized in the United States by writers such as Ralph Waldo Emerson and Henry David Thoreau, and many of those who were attracted to it lived a communitarian way of life. Perhaps the most famous Transcendentalist community was the experiment called Brook Farm, begun in New England by George Ripley.

Much influenced by this movement was Orestes Brownson. Sidney Ahlstrom, in his *Religious History of the American People*, describes Brownson as "a self-educated spiritual wanderer from rural Vermont whose pilgrimage brought him to the

Church of Rome at the age of forty-two—but by a notoriously winding route".[1]

Brownson was born into a Vermont family whose members ardently sought religious truth. It does not appear that any family member ever formally joined a church, but by age fourteen young Brownson was able to quote extensively from Genesis to Revelation. He felt the need to join a denomination that would give structure to his beliefs and, he hoped, challenge the power of his intellect. In the early 1820s, he became a Presbyterian, but soon left that denomination, maintaining that it imposed beliefs on its members and did not encourage thought. How, he argued, could one truly believe a series of propositions if one had not reasoned them out to his own satisfaction? To do that, he relied on reason alone for several years, but, without the guidance of some church structure, he found this insufficient also. Brownson thought the Universalist ministry might be what he was searching for, but when he could not find universal salvation clearly taught in the Bible, he likewise decided to abandon that path.

Utopian socialism was his next attraction—a purely secularist approach to life in which kindness, honesty, and personal betterment are stressed. It may be that the absence of any theological base at this time led him to a preoccupation with politics, specifically the New York Workingman's Party. He feared the excesses of capitalism, not the least of which was free trade.

> [T]he system which gives the supremacy to trade and manufacturers ... I regarded, and still regard [it], as worse than the serfdom of the middle ages, and worse even

---

[1] Sydney E. Ahlstrom, *A Religious History of the American People* (New Haven and London: Yale University Press, 1972), 549.

than slavery as it has existed or can exist in any Christian country.[2]

Within a decade of his first try at Presbyterianism, Brownson formed a friendship with William Ellery Channing, the famous Unitarian preacher, and he soon found himself preaching in Unitarian pulpits. At the same time, he began reading works by French and German philosophers and was introduced to a principal theorist of the concept of progress, Benjamin Constant. Further, he studied Pierre Leroux and thought him "the ablest and most original philosopher France has produced".[3] From Leroux he became convinced "that human life and thought is a 'joint product of subject and object' ".[4]

With the idea of communion with God firmly established in his mind, Brownson experienced a significant evolution in his personal thinking. Communion with God, he came to believe, would best be found in the life of Christ, the mediator between God and man. Christ could be discovered, not so much on one's own, but through an ecclesial body; and, finally, putting aside the prejudices with which he was raised, he had to conclude that Christ could be found completely in the body He had begun—the one, holy, catholic, and apostolic Church. It was that Church into which he was received on October 20, 1844, by Bishop John B. Fitzpatrick, coadjutor bishop of Boston.

In 1857, Brownson told his story in a work titled *The Convert*. He hoped it would bring others to the Church, but at the same time he let it be known the methods the Church was using to attract converts were, in his view, insufficient. To

[2] Orestes Brownson, cited in Patrick Allitt, *Catholic Converts: British and American Intellectuals Turn to Rome* (Ithaca: Cornell University Press, 1997), 65.

[3] Brownson, cited in Ahlstrom, op. cit., 550.

[4] Ibid.

those outside the Faith, the Catholic Church appeared intolerant, and little seemed to be done within the Church to correct that impression. He admitted that, prior to his conversion, he had taken a dim view of the Faith and the people who professed it: "I should sooner have thought of turning Jew, Mahometan, Gentoo, or Buddhist." [5]

Furthermore, he wrote, works written in defense of the Faith employed

> a dry, feeble, and unattractive style and abounded with terms and locutions which were to me totally unintelligible. Their authors seemed to me ignorant of the ideas and wants of the non-Catholic world, engrossed in obsolete questions, and wanting in broad and comprehensive views. [6]

Having lived and studied the Faith, Brownson ventured the opinion that, far from hindering one's mental queries, Catholicism was intellectually liberating. He recognized that a Catholic's mind, when used with intelligence,

> is no more restricted in its freedom by the authoritative dimensions of an infallible church than the cautious mariner by the charts and beacons that guide his course. [7]

Some years before his conversion, he had begun *Brownson's Quarterly Review*, a scholarly journal of opinion. When he became a Catholic, the tone of the journal changed dramatically. In its defense of Catholic teaching, it seemed to many to assume a strong apologetic tone. Brownson began to criticize many of the people he had once admired, and they quickly dropped him from being one of the heroes of the Transcendental Movement.

Unfortunately, Brownson began to use the pages of his

[5] Brownson, cited in Allitt, op. cit., 64.
[6] Ibid.
[7] Ibid.

review to criticize the very people with whom he should have had the strongest spiritual bond. He decried the "Irish Rabble", he accused the pope of being a despot in his temporal role of governing the Papal States, and he embraced the concept of Americanism, which some in the Church considered heretical. Many Catholic bishops became alarmed at his writings, and nowhere was this truer than in New York, where Archbishop John Hughes continually spoke up when he thought Brownson to be in error.

While Brownson could always be described as an independent thinker, with the passing of years he tended more toward defending the Faith and less toward criticizing those within its household. This change may be due to the influence of the Italian theologian and philosopher Vincenzo Gioberti, who was known for his keen apologetics, and whom Brownson considered "certainly one of the profoundest philosophical writers of this century". [8]

During the regional controversy preceding the Civil War, Brownson took a strong pro-Southern stance. It was only during the presidential campaign of 1860 that his thinking altered and he began to advance an anti-slavery unionist position. His writing began to resemble the abolitionist rhetoric of the day, causing a great deal of concern to Archbishop Hughes and other Northern bishops, who not only favored the more cautious approach of the Lincoln administration but knew all too well the anti-Catholicism of the abolitionists.

In his study *Catholic Converts: British and American Intellectuals Turn to Rome*, Patrick Allitt draws some valid comparisons and contrasts between Brownson and England's John Henry Newman:

---

[8] Brownson, cited in Ahlstrom, op. cit., 551.

1. Both men converted after many years of reading, study, and serious thought about what they had read and studied.

2. Brownson and Newman were also alike in their attempts to separate Catholicism from what they thought was an undue obsession with the Middle Ages. Linking the Church too specifically with one place or time could imply that she would not fit in with other places and times.

3. Each man also took a position that resulted in a bit of difficulty with his superiors: each thought that Catholic arts and sciences would gain greater respectability outside Church circles if scholars could work free of ecclesiastical interference. Patrick Allitt notes Newman even asserted that

> [t]here need be no harm in using books written by Protestants or skeptics, so long as they were not designed to undermine faith. After all, "the gravest Fathers recommended for Christian youth the use of pagan masters." [9]

There were, of course, contrasts:

1. Newman, an Anglican vicar, wanted to bring to life a church he thought was on the verge of extinction and to bring an end to its subordination to the state. He took a vow of celibacy early on, and his life as a professor centered him in the university town of Oxford.

2. Brownson, a married man with a large family, traveled extensively in his various professions and held many differing convictions prior to his conversion.[10]

One of the American converts strongly influenced by Brownson was a son of German Lutheran immigrants who was born

[9] Allitt, op. cit., 79.
[10] Each of these points and several others are elaborated in greater detail in Allitt, op. cit., 74–84.

in 1819 and grew up in New York City, anguished, we are told, by religious doubt; his name was Isaac Hecker.

Hecker as a young man had briefly been a member of the Methodist church. A meeting with Brownson in 1841 led to a lengthy correspondence between the two, in which Brownson tried to give some direction to Hecker's religious search by recommending certain authors who had greatly helped him in his own journey. In addition to such reading, Hecker early on displayed a desire for community life, by spending time first at Bronson Alcott's vegetarian commune and then at George Ripley's Brook Farm, the Transcendental commune in New England. In later years, he was to describe Brook Farm as "the greatest, noblest, bravest dream of New England" and "the realization of the best dreams [its founders] had of Christianity".[11]

Hecker actually preceded Brownson into the Church by a few months, though Brownson's decision to become a Catholic is thought to have been a considerable influence on Hecker. Once in the Church, Hecker decided to enter the Congregation of the Most Holy Redeemer, more popularly, the Redemptorists. The community had been founded in Italy in the previous century by Saint Alphonsus Liguori to work among poor people. In the United States, their earliest apostolate was the care of German immigrants, and Hecker, with his German background, must have felt a particular affinity with these people. He left for the Netherlands to enter the novitiate and was joined by two other recent converts, Clarence Walworth and James Alphonsus McMaster. Both were former Episcopalians, and, of the three, Hecker and Walworth were ordained. McMaster returned to New York to become the controversial editor of the *Freeman's Journal*, a

---

[11] Hecker, cited in Allitt, op. cit., 68.

publication that at times was the official organ of the arch-bishop of New York.

Hecker returned to the United States in 1851 and immediately joined the Redemptorist mission band, where he achieved great renown as a preacher. He became so well known that at one point he found himself among three possible candidates to be appointed bishop of Natchez, Mississippi.

In the midst of all this, he began to perceive what he considered serious defects in his congregation. Redemptorist houses still retained an Old World European style, speaking the German language. Hecker thought the time had come to assimilate into the American culture by speaking English and changing the outreach of the Redemptorists from immigrants to non-Catholic Americans.

Father Hecker found himself head of a group of Redemptorists who also felt this way, and he acted as spokesman when the group traveled to Rome to discuss these matters with the superior general. Rather than having a sympathetic ear, the general was of a totally different mind-set. Father Hecker was dismissed from the congregation on charges of disobedience; specifically, not obtaining the required permission to make the European voyage. Friends in the papal curia secured for Hecker and his companions dispensation from their Redemptorist vows and permission to organize a new religious community with a specific apostolate to Protestant America.

Upon Hecker's return in 1858, Archbishop Hughes of New York approved the rule that had been drawn up and that was, in many ways, similar to that of the Redemptorists. The new community was to be called the Congregation of Missionary Priests of Saint Paul the Apostle, known more popularly as the Paulist Fathers. To this day the order is responsible for a parish in New York City. The church, located on 59th Street, near Central Park and Columbus Circle, is one of the more beautiful and well-known churches in Manhattan.

In 1865, the year the Civil War ended, Hecker and his associates founded the *Catholic World*. Following that, they began a Tract Society to distribute well-written apologetic literature to non-Catholics. Their style was not to attack Protestant America or even to challenge it but, rather, to bring the consoling message of the fullness of the truth.

This was not a new approach for Isaac Hecker; he had done it ten years earlier when he wrote a book called *Questions of the Soul*. He investigated Catholic claims and vindicated them one by one. He concluded, for example, that

> [t]he Pope was not a tyrant, for he was subject to Catholic doctrines like everyone else. . . . Confessing one's sins to a priest was laudable, superior to the American alternative of confessional popular literature with all its "filthy and disgust-ing details," which polluted the minds of innocents. . . . The priest preserved the seal of the confessional, while administer-ing divine forgiveness to penitents; society and the individual soul both benefited. Monasticism was an option for those who sought to free themselves from the bondage of the self; mortification prompted charity; chastity and poverty nur-tured holiness; and the cult of the saints gave earthly glimpses of heaven.[12]

None of this is to suggest that Hecker did not refute the claims of other branches of Christianity and that he did not try to show the error of their reasoning; but he did so calmly, with well-reasoned arguments, and always with great charity.

Father Hecker did invite controversy; some thought him a minimalist in doctrinal matters, others thought him a Mod-ernist. Strong cases can be made against both charges, but, in

---

[12] Ibid., 70.

fact, these charges were made. Some years after his death, a fellow Paulist, Father Walter Elliott, wrote his biography, and a French translation of this book seemed to portray Hecker as saying that active virtues were more important than passive ones, religious vows should be deemphasized, and more stress should be laid on the direct working of the Holy Spirit in individual souls. These ideas led to the so-called heresy of Americanism. Some thought it a phantom heresy; others considered it a serious threat. Leo XIII thought it significant enough to intervene with *Testem Benevolentiae*, an apostolic letter to the church of the United States.

One of the great contributions of Father Hecker's community in the United States was the establishment in 1902 of the Apostolic Mission House at Catholic University of America in Washington, D.C. Its purpose was to train Paulist Fathers in their work of making converts among non-Catholics. No one will ever fully know the good done, the converts made, all because one convert, Isaac Hecker, saw the compatibility between Catholicism and American life.

7

ROBERT HUGH BENSON AND
C. C. MARTINDALE

Two of England's best-known priests

A visit to England for many people should include a stop in the beautiful medieval city of Canterbury. The city is noted for its magnificent cathedral, the pilgrimage site for the travelers in Chaucer's *Canterbury Tales*, as well as the site, two centuries earlier, of the martyrdom of Thomas à Becket. The word *cathedral* derives from the Latin *cathedra*, "seat". A cathedral church is one presided over by a bishop. At the time of the Protestant Reformation, this particular cathedral became the seat of the archbishop of Canterbury, the head of the Church of England, a position of very high visibility. Given that background, the conversion of the son of an archbishop of Canterbury to the Roman Catholic Faith would be a newsworthy event indeed. And such a conversion did take place. Robert Hugh Benson, son of Edward White Benson, an archbishop of Canterbury, became a Catholic in 1903, then a priest in 1904, and eventually he was named a monsignor.

Hugh Benson was born in 1871 into a family that proved to be very literary. His brother E. F. Benson was a popular novelist and writer of memoirs. Arthur Benson, another brother, spent an academic career at Magdalene College, Cambridge, and Hugh himself became famous for mastering the art of religious disputation. His prep-school education was at Eton; then followed Trinity College, Cambridge. Many think his strongest motive for taking orders in the Anglican Church—even stronger than his religious fervor—was to please his father.

His father, the archbishop, conferred orders upon Hugh in 1894, and he was assigned to a poor parish near London, Hackney Wick. He had not been there very long when his father died suddenly. The archbishop had gone to pay a visit to Prime Minister William Gladstone and died during the visit, while on his knees, praying. His funeral, as one might imagine, was one of great national pageantry, and Hugh played an active role in the ritual, reading a lengthy litany of petitions for his father.

But the emotional strain of his father's death took its toll, and his superiors instructed Hugh to spend the winter months in Egypt. It was a trip that would have great impact on his future. By discovering how inconsequential the Church of England was outside England, Benson began to wonder about a church that lacked universality. It struck him first in the predominantly Catholic countries of the Continent: "Behold, we were nowhere in this vast continent; it apparently was ignorant of our existence." [1]

Once he arrived in Egypt, another grace was given him. He happened into a small, humble Catholic church, one that stood in the midst of mud houses where poor inhabitants lived. Benson said that there he began to feel the presence of God. Our Lord's Real Presence in the Blessed Sacrament was somehow made manifest to him, though he was not fully

[1] Robert Hugh Benson, cited in Rawley Myers, *Faith Experiences of Catholic Converts* (Huntington, Ind.: Our Sunday Visitor, 1992), 75.

aware of it. "It had a singularly uninviting interior",[2] he noted, but how vastly different it stood in comparison to many Anglican cathedrals, which, he said, reminded him of museums.

Benson had no idea the Lord was leading him to the fullness of truth. In fact, he looked forward to the trip's ending, so that no further difficulties would present themselves. From Egypt, he went to the Holy Land, where he read in a British newspaper about an Anglican minister, a man he knew and respected, becoming a Roman Catholic. "It is impossible to describe the horror and shock that this was to me."[3]

Benson's return to England found him serving as an assistant in a parish in Kemsing, Kent. It was an enjoyable assignment for a time, until the doubts he experienced on his travels began to surface again. Why did every Anglican bishop seem to be saying different things? How was it possible for the Catholic Church to have deceived people for centuries before the Reformation? Such questions plagued him, and he decided to leave the active ministry to join an Anglican religious community, the Community of the Resurrection. Not unlike men in Catholic monastic life, these men worked, prayed, and studied together, living communally. It was there that Benson began praying the Rosary daily and from there that he went out to Anglican parishes, preaching and establishing a considerable reputation.

His personal holiness was enhanced tremendously by the experience, but his faith in his creed was not. He wrote to a prominent Catholic priest, explaining in detail his struggles and why it was becoming more difficult to remain an Anglican. The priest wrote back, encouraging him to stay where he was. His advice gave Benson some peace of mind, until he

[2] Ibid.
[3] Ibid.

later read that the same priest had abandoned his priesthood and left the Church.[4]

In his intellectual journey to the Faith, Benson was greatly helped by Cardinal Newman's *Essay on the Development of Christian Doctrine*, Mallock's *Doctrine and Doctrinal Disruption*, and even a book by an Anglican, Spencer Jones, *England and the Holy See*. From his study of Scripture he came upon a statement Saint Jerome had made: "I am in communion with the Chair of Peter. On this Rock I know the Church is built." [5]

How could one truly believe in Christ, Benson thought, and not follow such a belief to its logical conclusion?

Some years after his reception into the Church, Hugh Benson wrote a wonderful memoir titled *Confessions of a Convert*. Looking back at those years of spiritual pilgrimage, he said that it was not scholarship that finally brought him to truth; rather, it was the path of humility and prayerfulness. Every day he meditated on the Three Degrees of Humility in the *Spiritual Exercises* of Saint Ignatius of Loyola. He recalled:

> Two or three texts of Scripture began to burn before me. "A highway shall be there," wrote Isaias; ". . . the redeemed shall walk there . . . the wayfaring men, though fools, shall not err therein." "A city set upon a hill", said our Savior, "cannot be hid." Again: "unless you become as little children you cannot enter into the Kingdom of heaven". And again: "I thank Thee Father, because Thou hast hid these things from the wise and prudent, and has revealed them to little ones." [6]

At that point, he wrote in his memoir, he took temporary leave from the Community of the Resurrection and went to

[4] Ibid., 76.

[5] Ibid., 77.

[6] Robert Hugh Benson, *Confessions of a Convert* (Sevenoaks, Kent: Fisher Press, 1991), 75–76.

his family home. He wanted to rest his mind from the religious turmoil that had been plaguing him for months, so he set himself to writing a novel, *By What Authority?* Actually, the writing of the novel proved to increase his difficulties all the more and to make more evident to him the errors of his ways:

> For years past I had claimed to be saying Mass, and that the sacrifice of the Mass was held as a doctrine by the Church of England; and here in Elizabethan days were priests hunted to death for the crime of doing that which I had claimed to do. I had supposed that our wooded Communion tables were altars, and here in Tudor times were the old stones of the altars defiled and insulted deliberately by the officials of the Church to which I still nominally belonged, and wooden tables substituted instead. Things which were dear to me . . . —vestments, crucifixes, rosaries—in Elizabethan days were denounced as trinkets and "monuments of superstition." I began to wonder at myself, and a little while later gave up celebrating the Communion service.[7]

Clearly, he was becoming more spiritually tormented. Some time later he took another step:

> I went on in despair and stayed a Sunday at lodgings at Chichester, where for the last time, in a little church opposite the cathedral, I made my Anglican confession, telling the clergyman plainly that I was practically certain that I should become a Roman Catholic. He very kindly gave me his absolution and told me to cheer up.[8]

Benson then contacted Father Reginald Buckler, a Dominican Father living at the friary at Woodchester. After taking instructions, Robert Hugh Benson was received into the Catholic Church:

[7] Ibid., 87.
[8] Ibid., 91.

On the Friday, the day fixed for my reception, I took a long, lonely walk, still entirely uninterested, and visited the Church of Minchinhampton, on the opposite side of the valley. I was caught in the rain, I remember, and had tea in a small public-house parlour, where there was a rather witty list of instructions to visitors as to the personal prowess of the landlord and his intentions of enforcing order. Then I came back to the Priory about six o'clock.[9]

He claimed not to have had any intense spiritual experience; all he did was get wet. "[T]here seemed nothing within me at all except an absolute certainty I was doing God's will." [10]

The year was 1903; he was thirty-two years of age. As to why he did not convert earlier in life, he said it was the wish of his mother and other family members that he should give himself every possible opportunity for a change of mind under new surroundings. Moreover, even though his own mental condition was such that he knew the Catholic Church was the true Church, he did not know that he knew, to paraphrase Cardinal Newman.

Benson received hundreds of letters after his conversion, but only three of them were from Catholics. The rest were from Anglicans—clergy, laymen and women, and even some children, "most of whom regarded me either as a deliberate traitor (but of these there were very few) or as an infatuated fool, or as an impatient, headstrong, ungrateful bigot".[11]

After a short period of study in Rome, Benson was ordained to the Catholic priesthood in 1904. The remainder of his life was devoted to preaching and writing. He worked for a time as chaplain to the Catholic undergraduates at Cambridge University. One of those students, Shane Leslie, would

[9] Ibid., 97.
[10] Benson, cited in Myers, op. cit., 78.
[11] Benson, op. cit., 100.

himself become a well-known convert to Catholicism, and, looking back on his undergraduate years, he recalled Father Benson's flamboyancy in communication:

> He mastered his stammer in the pulpit by convulsions and gestures. It was difficult to say if he were wrestling with his stammer or with Satan. He would begin slowly, anxiously, as though he had a secret, and from the moment he possessed his audience he ceased to keep his possession of himself. He gave the feeling that he was preaching his last sermon on the eve of the Day of Judgment. He began to mop his brow, he waved his arms and his eyes stared out of his face in agony. He seemed to fall back into convulsions, and to collapse out of the pulpit, whence he was led into a hot bath.[12]

Monsignor Benson became well known in the United States; a number of preaching tours sharpened his perception of the Catholic Church in this country. He felt that it

> inspires the visitor from Europe with an extraordinary sense of life; the churches are not exquisite sanctuaries for dreaming—they are the business offices of the supernatural; the clergy are not picturesque advocates of a beautiful medievalism—they are keen and devoted to the service of God; the people are not pathetic survivals from the Ages of Faith—they are communities of immortal souls bent upon salvation. There is a ring of assurance about Catholic voices, an air of confidence about Catholic movements . . . a swing and energy about Catholic life, that promise well indeed for the future of the Church in this land.[13]

In the course of his brief life, Monsignor Benson wrote fifteen novels; several collections of stories; a book of poems,

---

[12] Shane Leslie, *Long Shadows*, as quoted in Patrick Allitt, *Catholic Converts: British and American Intellectuals Turn to Rome* (Ithaca: Cornell University Press, 1997), 281.

[13] Benson, cited in Allitt, op. cit., 282.

devotional writing, and apologetics; sermons and essays; and several plays for children. He died of pneumonia in 1914, soon after volunteering to go to the front as a military chaplain in the First World War. His life spanned only forty-two years, but how much he put into those years.

Robert Hugh Benson has been the subject of several books and specialized studies through the years, but perhaps his best-known biographer was the Jesuit convert Cyril Charles Martindale, affectionately known to the literary, scholarly, and Catholic devotional world as C. C. Martindale.

C. C. Martindale was born in 1879, only eight years after Hugh Benson, but he lived nearly twice as long, dying in the early 1960s, when he was into his eighties.

Martindale attended Harrow, a famous prep school, and while there, at the age of fourteen, he converted to Catholicism. On leaving school, he joined the Jesuits, who sent him to Oxford. His accomplishments there were many: the Hertford prize, the Craven scholarship, the Latin and Greek prize, the Derby scholarship, the Ellerton theological prize; and twice he was runner-up for the Ireland scholarship. Those who knew him assumed that his university career would be exceptional and that a scholarly life would follow. In fact, something very different happened.

World War I brought a number of wounded Australian soldiers to Oxford. Martindale spent every spare moment he could with them, and that contact was decisive. He saw that his special vocation lay not with scholars but with ordinary people.

Father Bernard Basset, one of the historians of the English Jesuits, wrote that young Martindale was

> entirely absorbed with the needs of the present moment, above all the need to bring the message of the Incarnation to

a suffering world. Classless, selfless, restless, his mind was for
ever composing variations on this central theme.[14]

Nor was his life limited to wounded soldiers. He also
worked with merchant seamen, for whom he helped to establish the Apostleship of the Sea. His interest in youth led him
to establish a center for them in the East End of London and
to spend a good deal of his time working with them. When
not at that type of work, he was producing well-remembered
books, such as *Christ the King, Gates of the Church, The Wounded
World, The Creative Words of Christ,* and *What Think You of
Christ?* He was even a radio pioneer, in the infant days of the
BBC, hosting a program titled *What Are Saints?*

Frank Sheed, Catholic publisher, apologist, and lay theologian, was a man upon whom Father Martindale had an enormous impact. Sheed, in his memoir *The Church and I,* tried to
describe Martindale's vision of the Church and how it had so
influenced his own view:

> The essence of it lay in a clear awareness of the distinction
> between Christ, who energizes in his members, and the mem-
> bers in the variousness of their response to Christ's energiz-
> ing. The clarity of his awareness of the contrast did not affect
> the totality of his submission to the commands either of the
> Church or his order.[15]

The faith to which Martindale converted as a boy is that of
the Church, to whom he gave his all. In 1921 he wrote:

> When your intelligence makes you able to do so, you ought
> to get a complete picture of your Faith, and of your home,
> the Church: You ought to see her as a whole, many-roomed,

---

[14] Bernard Basset, S.J., *The English Jesuits: From Campion to Martindale* (London: Burns and Oates, 1967; New York: Herder and Herder, 1968), 452.
[15] Frank Sheed, *The Church and I* (Garden City, N.Y.: Doubleday, 1974),
116.

yet entirely inter-connected in all her parts; and you ought never fall victim to the boasts of rationalism, which assures you that much of your belief is badly founded, propped by tottering walls, leakily roofed, or a mere labyrinth with no centre, and no clue. It has been my almost invariable experience, when I have met a man who has left, or is leaving, the Church, that along with other reasons, this has been one—he has never understood what he is leaving.[16]

Certainly C. C. Martindale was a man of the people. The many popular books he wrote to attract people to Catholicism are great proof of this fact. Father Basset characterized him well:

Certainly he was devoted to his Order and was greatly admired by all. Yet, he was always too absorbed to bother about exclusively Jesuit undertakings and saw no problem in shedding the middle-class trappings of the Victorian world.[17]

Maisie Ward, Frank Sheed's wife and publishing partner, was also a friend of Father Martindale. She once remarked that he carried to a high point that struggle between other people's needs and his own personal fulfillment. And Maisie adds that he once told her husband of his rule never to refuse to do anything he was asked to do if it could fit into his time. In a letter to Maisie he wrote:

I know . . . that I disappointed many people by not becoming an expert in something or other of a "scholarly" sort. But really, the only thing that ever "captured" me was people. Even while I "ground at grammar" at Oxford, I kept feeling more and more that I was meeting real persons.[18]

[16] C. C. Martindale, S.J., *The Gates of the Church* (New York: Sheed and Ward, 1936), 23–24.

[17] Basset, *The English Jesuits*, 452.

[18] Martindale to Maisie Ward, cited in Maisie Ward, *Unfinished Business* (London: Sheed and Ward, 1964), 361.

No one will ever know how many persons were touched by him: in his apostolates, in his writing, through his preaching, by his apologetics. He may not have been an expert in one scholarly area, but one suspects he was an expert in the most important thing, winning souls for Christ though His Church.

8

EDITH STEIN

Jewish Carmelite Sister Teresa Benedicta

The story of the Jewish Carmelite Sister Teresa Benedicta of the Cross, known in the world as Edith Stein, presents us with one of the more brilliant converts to come to the Faith in this century; it also places us in close contact with a horrendous tragedy of the modern world, the Holocaust.

Edith Stein was born on October 12, 1891, in Breslau, Germany. Her birthplace was rich in history:

> Breslau . . . is equidistant from the borders which, in her time, marked Poland and Bohemia. The Jews of this area were in large part descended from the merchant Jews of the early Middle Ages who joined migrants from Central Europe and took refuge in Bohemia and Poland during the years of the Crusades.[1]

Edith was the youngest of eleven children in a Jewish family that observed the major religious feasts but did not appear to have been overly zealous in the practice of their faith. It was a family that knew sorrow. Four of the children died young, and the father, who owned a lumber business, died quite suddenly at age forty-eight, leaving his widow with

[1] The citation is from the translator's Afterword of Sister Josephine Koeppel, O.C.D., in Dr. L. Gelber and Romaeus Leuven, O.C.D., eds., *The Collected Works of Edith Stein* (Washington, D.C.: ICS Publications, 1986), 1:447.

many debts. These factors may have accounted for Edith's leaving school for a time at age thirteen. It is also possible that a loss of religious faith accounted for her leaving. For eight years, she claimed to have no belief in a personal God, though there can be no doubt that same God, hidden from her for whatever reason, was drawing her to Himself through the world of philosophy.

In 1913, at age twenty-two, she left her native Breslau (now Wrocław, Poland) to begin studies at the University of Göttingen in Germany. The university was renowned as a center for a rising new philosophical movement called phenomenology. It was attracting the best and brightest phenomenologists, and overshadowing them all was the figure of Edmund Husserl. In 1900 Husserl had published a work called *Logical Investigations*. He thought that philosophy as a discipline was becoming too absorbed in the world of psychology; when this happened it became harder and harder for philosophy to concentrate on the great issues, such as the nature of man, the world, and religious experience. To counter that tendency, Husserl developed the phenomenological method.

For Husserl, the proper study of philosophy was the object (philosophy had become too subjective; Husserl believed that when we study philosophy we study objects). Knowledge for Husserl was always knowledge of something. There is always an object of our knowledge, yet the object of knowledge was not exactly the thing itself. All objects must be "bracketed", put into parentheses, thus forcing one to view the object in a pure state. Detached from the world of experience, the object then presents itself to our insight in all its essential purity. Such was phenomenology.

Edith entered this world at the University of Göttingen. She had been aware of Edmund Husserl for a long time and would now have opportunity to study under him. She was attracted to the realistic nature of his philosophy, grounded as it was in metaphysics. In addition to Husserl, Edith was fascinated by the lectures of Max Scheler, a Jewish philosopher who was to convert to Catholicism in 1920. (There can be little doubt that Scheler, by his stirring presentation of the spiritual beauty of Catholicism, led many of Husserl's disciples to consider their spiritual poverty and to move in the direction of the Catholic Church.)

In 1916, Husserl asked Edith to be his teaching assistant and to go with him to Freiburg, where he had accepted a professorship. At the time, Edith was writing her doctoral dissertation "On the Problem of Empathy", for which she received her degree summa cum laude. She also began putting Husserl's early writings in order.

Not long after this, Edith took a significant step in her faith journey. She attended the funeral of a young married man, a Christian, with whom she had become friendly. She was amazed that the young man's widow, far from being visibly overcome with grief, seemed more concerned with consoling others in their sorrow. What could possibly account for such peace of soul? Edith decided the answer might lie in the New Testament, and she began to read it. From this reading, the presence of God became more personal to her.

One day Edith was talking with a friend and fellow phenomenologist, Hans Lipps. He began telling her about people like Dietrich von Hildebrand, Siegfried Hamburger, and other phenomenologists who had converted to Catholicism, and, somewhat jokingly, he said to her, "You haven't joined that club of people who go to Mass every day in Munich, have you?" "Oh, no", she replied. That was 1916; her decision to enter the Catholic Church was still six years away.

By 1918, Edith had returned to Breslau, where she tutored students privately. She began reading Kierkegaard, but she was not particularly moved by his idea that one must make a "leap of faith". To her, that idea seemed to separate faith from the use of one's mind. Instead, she began reading meditations on the Gospels, and she wondered if she might follow her mentor, Husserl, into the Lutheran Church.

She would not. A chance reading of the autobiography of Saint Teresa of Avila ensured her taking a very different route. She was visiting friends in Bergzabern and one evening came upon the book in their library. She became totally absorbed and believed she had at last arrived at truth.

> What Edith Stein found in Teresa's autobiography was the confirmation of her own experience. God is not a God of knowledge, God is love. He does not reveal his mysteries to the deductive intelligence, but to the heart that surrenders itself to him. Along with being a mystic, Teresa of Avila was also a born psychologist and teacher of self-knowledge. Through her combination of mystical ardor and practical pedagogy, she succeeded in overcoming Edith Stein's "metaphysical prejudices" as well as her fear of encountering God.[2]

If Edith had never attended a Catholic Mass, she did now, in the parish church of Bergzabern. One can only guess at the surprise of the priest when she came back to the sacristy following Mass and asked to be received into the Church. The priest explained to her the normal course of instruction that usually preceded such a reception, and he must have experienced even greater surprise when, upon Edith's request that he examine her on the Faith, found her knowledge to be more than sufficient. The date for her baptism was fixed: New Year's Day, 1922.

---

[2] Waltraud Herbstrith, O.C.D., *Edith Stein: A Biography* (San Francisco: Ignatius Press, 1992), 65. See also Rawley Myers, *Faith Experiences of Catholic Converts* (Huntington, Ind.: Our Sunday Visitor, 1992), 94.

One student whom Edith tutored, who became a professor of philosophy herself, has left an interesting memoir of the aftermath of Edith's conversion:

> Hard as she tried to spare her mother pain, her mother understood this passionately loved child of hers better than Edith knew. I remember Edith telling me once that she always went to early Mass so that she could be home before anyone noticed it, and her mother telling me afterward with bitter tears that she had always heard the door close, no matter how quietly Edith left the house, and that she knew that it had to be Edith going off to Church. . . . Mother and daughter loved each other devotedly. Edith Stein wanted nothing more than to be a good daughter to her mother, and this remained true after she set out on her appointed path.[3]

For the next eight years, Edith lived with the Dominicans in Speyer, teaching at Saint Magdalene's, a training institute for teachers. She had put aside the rigors of the scholarly life, but Saint Magdalene's initiated her into the rigors of convent life, for it was that sort of life that attracted her from the beginning, specifically, the life of Carmel, which Saint Teresa of Avila had lived.

As Edith tells it in her own words:

> Initially, when I was baptized on New Year's Day, 1922, I thought of it as a preparation for entrance in the Order. But a few months later, when I saw my mother for the first time after the baptism, I realized that she couldn't handle another blow for the present. Not that it would have killed her—but I couldn't have held myself responsible for the embitterment it would have caused.[4]

---

[3] Edith Stein Archives, Cologne Carmel, Germany, cited in Herbstrith, op. cit., 71.

[4] Teresia Renata Posselt, *Edith Stein: Eine Grosse Frau unseres Jahrhunderts*, 9th ed. (Freiburg, Basel, Vienna: Herder, 1963), 100, cited in Herbstrith, op. cit. 73.

Curiously, after her conversion, she continued to accompany her mother to the synagogue. As the Jewish people prayed the Psalms of the Old Testament, Edith recited those same Psalms from a Roman Rite breviary she took with her. If her mother's observation is correct, Edith's spirituality must have been intense; Frau Stein claimed never to have seen anyone else pray the way her daughter prayed.[5]

In 1925, Edith encountered yet another strong influence in her life in the presence of the Jesuit Erich Pryzwara. He was a very powerful presence in European Catholic circles, and his thought had a great influence on other theologians, including Hans Urs von Balthasar. Father Pryzwara convinced Edith not only to make a serious study of Saint Thomas Aquinas but also to translate his work *De Veritate*. For someone like Edith, who had been trained in phenomenology, this was not an easy task. Phenomenologists treat only the object: any serious study of the same should be unencumbered by other commentary. Saint Thomas Aquinas, on the other hand, quoted from the Fathers, the Doctors of the Church, Jewish commentators, Greek philosophers, unbelievers, and saints.

Despite that difference, Edith wrote another manuscript, comparing Husserl with Aquinas. Both sought a precise method of thinking and a certain body of truths; both engaged in philosophy as a serious pursuit, not as a pastime; neither doubted the power of reason, although Aquinas seemed to give it greater scope when he included supernatural knowledge. By drawing out these and other similarities between the two philosophers, Edith made a unique contribution to the philosophical world.

The intensity of prayer that Edith's mother had observed in her continued to develop. Retreats contributed to the quality

[5] See ibid., 74.

of that prayer. Edith Stein's desire increased for the religious life, specifically, the life of Carmel, to which she had been so drawn from her reading of Saint Teresa of Avila. Naturally, her family's reaction was one of much concern, but, by 1933, Edith knew that the time had come; and, once her decision was made, she began to experience the peace of Christ as never before.[6]

In her writings, Edith has left us a poignant account of her last day at home before entering Carmel:

> [M]y mother buried her face in her hands and began to cry. I stood behind her chair, resting her old white-haired head against my chest. We stayed like that for a long time, until I was able to convince her to go up to bed. After taking her upstairs and helping her to undress—for the first time in her life—I sat alongside her at the edge of the bed until she sent me off to sleep. But I don't think either one of us got any sleep that night.[7]

Her new life in the Carmel of Cologne, Germany, was a lesson in humility. To most of the young sisters, Edith was simply an older postulant. As they had no idea of her intellectual past or of her accomplishments, they did not seek counsel from her any more than they would from another newcomer. In the midst of this, she was sustained by an ideal expressed by Teresa of Avila, an ideal Edith herself developed in an article she wrote about the saint:

> Only the person who renounces self-importance, who no longer struggles to defend or assert himself, can be large enough for God's boundless action.[8]

---

[6] Myers, *Faith Experiences of Catholic Converts*, 95.

[7] Herbstrith, op. cit., 122.

[8] Edith Stein, "Eine Meisterin der Erziehungs- und Bildundsarbeit: Teresia von Jesus", in *Katholische Frauenbildung im deutschen Volk*, 48 (February, 1935): 122–23, cited in Herbstrith, op. cit., 128.

One of the great spiritual influences on her during her earliest days at the Carmel was the autobiography of her fellow Carmelite Saint Thérèse of Lisieux, *The Story of a Soul.* After reading it, Edith wrote,

> My impression was, that this was a life which had been absolutely transformed by the love of God, down to the last detail. I simply can't imagine anything greater. I would like to see this attitude incorporated as much as possible into my own life and the lives of those who are dear to me.[9]

In the Carmel, after the taking of her first vows, she was known as Sister Teresa Benedicta of the Cross. Her thankfulness to two saints and her absorption in Christ's Passion both found expression in her name and title.

> Would you like to know my patron [she wrote to Mother Petra]? It's obviously holy Father Benedict. Even though I never even became a Benedictine Oblate—since all I could ever see ahead of me was Mount Carmel—he's been kind enough to adopt me and to make me an honorary member of his order.[10]

During her years in the cloister, she remained true to her literary output, and some of her writings directly engaged those outside this world of contemplation:

> There's quite a distance between leading the self-satisfied existence of the "good Catholic" who "does his duty", "reads the right newspaper", and "votes correctly"—and then does just as he pleases—and living one's life in the presence of God, with the simplicity of a child, and the humility of the

---

[9] Edith Stein, *Selbstbildnis in Briefen*, I. Teil, 1916–1934, Edith Steins Werke, Bd. VIII (Druten: De Maas and Waler; Freiburg, Basel, Vienna: Herder, 1976), Letter 137, p. 133, cited in Herbstrith, op. cit., 123–24.

[10] Ibid., II, Letter 178, p. 13, cited in Herbstrith, op. cit., 130.

publican. But I can assure you: once anyone has taken the first step, he won't want to turn back.[11]

In her writings, Edith continually developed the theme that Christ's sacrifice on the Cross and the Holy Sacrifice of the Mass are in fact one and the same sacrifice. From her religious background, she knew the importance of sacrificial prayer for Old Testament prophets. At a given moment in time, however, Jesus Christ offered a very different type of sacrifice. Because he was the God-man, the sacrifice of His body on the Cross was the one perfect sacrifice, replacing all that had gone before. It was His perfect prayer to His heavenly Father, and about that prayer Edith added a further thought:

> Jesus did more than merely participate in officially prescribed liturgical worship. Perhaps with even greater frequency the Gospels show him praying alone in the silence of the night, on open hills, or in uninhabited deserts. They speak of him praying for forty days and nights before beginning his public ministry, retreating into mountain solitudes before choosing and commissioning his apostles, preparing himself at Gethsemane for the journey to Golgotha.[12]

By 1938, the situation had become so difficult for the Jewish people in Germany that Edith knew that if she did not leave Cologne she would be placing the lives of all the sisters in the convent in jeopardy. Edith's sister Rosa had also become a Catholic and was living the life of a laywoman in the Carmel. The two of them left Cologne for Echt, Holland. The Carmel in that town was to be their home for the next four years.

---

[11] Edith Stein, "Weihnachtsgeheimnis", in *Wege zur inneren Stille*, collected articles, ed. W. Herbstrith (Frankfurt: Kafka Verlag, 1978), 22–24, cited in Herbstrith, op. cit., 154.

[12] Ibid., 33–34, cited in Herbstrith, op. cit., 155.

As Hitler's forces occupied neighboring countries, the goal of Jewish extermination became even more pronounced, and this "vast network of death" was extended not only against Jews but against Jewish converts to other creeds. The Nazis dared not move against Catholic Church leaders for fear of recrimination. Jews who had become Catholics, however, were another matter in the Nazis' thinking. S.S. operations were extended to seize all such Jews, and specifically those found in religious orders. When news of this became public, Edith realized her lot in Holland would be no better than it had been in Germany. She and Rosa applied for Swiss visas, hoping to escape to the Carmel in Le Paquier. The difficulty was a shortage of accommodations. The Carmel could take Edith but not her sister. Edith refused to leave her, and, although they remained in Holland, their visa application was never formally withdrawn.

At five o'clock on the evening of August 2, 1942, two S.S. officers arrived at the door of the Echt Carmel demanding to see Edith Stein. The superior thought little of it, believing all they wanted was to speak to Edith about her pending visa. Upon entering the convent parlor, Edith was told she and Rosa had only minutes to pack their belongings. Frau Bromberg, a fellow prisoner with Edith, retained a vivid recollection of her. It was in the detention camp, as they were awaiting deportation.

> What distinguished Edith Stein from the rest of the sisters was her silence. Rather than seeming fearful, to me she appeared deeply oppressed. . . . She hardly ever spoke; but often she would look at her sister Rosa with a sorrow beyond words. As I write, it occurs to me that she probably understood what was awaiting them.[13]

---

[13] Posselt, 214, cited in Herbstrith, op. cit., 182.

Later, when the official Dutch *Gazette* published the names of all Jews who had been deported from Holland on August 7, 1942, the following entry was included:

> Number 44074, Edith Theresia Hedwig Stein, Echt
> Born—October 12, 1891, Breslau
> Died—August 9, 1942[14]

On October 11, 1998, fifty-six years, two months, and two days after her death at Auschwitz, Edith Stein, Sister Teresa Benedicta of the Cross, was canonized a saint of the Roman Catholic Church by Pope John Paul II.

---

[14] Herbstrith, op. cit., 190.

9

GILBERT KEITH CHESTERTON

Innocence and humility

G. K. Chesterton once sent his wife what has become a famous telegram: "Am in market Harborough: where ought I to be?" If there is truth in the observation that absentmindedness is a sign of genius, it is certainly borne out in this man's life. C. S. Lewis called him "the most sensible man alive". T. S. Eliot was keenly aware of the importance of the Catholic Church on the world scene, and he felt Chesterton had done more to bring that importance to light than any other man of his time. Converts such as Monsignor Ronald Knox and historian Theodore Maynard credited Chesterton with playing an indispensable role in their conversions.[1]

Chesterton's ability to demonstrate brilliance in so many areas accounts for his long-standing appeal. To some he was an essayist. To others, a novelist. To still others, a poet or writer of detective stories. Many enjoyed his works of history, theology, or politics. Whether an audience heard him lecture, engage in debate, or speak on radio, the reaction he elicited from them ranged from admiration to resentment. Such is true of all public men, but this public man was always scintillating, never boring. His chief rivals were the first to respect

[1] Kevin Morris, *G. K. Chesterton: A Great Catholic* (London: Catholic Truth Society, 1994), 8.

his talent for literacy expressiveness, a talent aptly shown in his account of the beginning of his life:

> Bowing down in blind credulity, as is my custom, before mere authority and the tradition of the elders, superstitiously swallowing a story I could not test at the time by experiment or private judgement, I am firmly of opinion that I was born on the 29th of May, 1874, on Campden Hill, Kensington.[2]

Gilbert and his brother, Cecil, younger by three years, were born into comfortable circumstances. Their father, Edward Chesterton, had inherited a family business from his father. Gilbert was sent to Saint Paul's, one of England's great private schools, centrally located in London and attracting some of the finest students in the country. Upon leaving school at age eighteen, he trained as an artist, then spent six years working for publishers and, finally, captivated by the lure of London's Fleet Street, settled on a career in journalism.

> He also passionately believed that he had something to say to the people, a moral message in a world going to the asylum if not to the dogs; the idea of Chesterton as a prophet is not far-fetched. Ideas cascaded from him . . . he literally worked himself to death in order to express joy in the world, and to help the poor and helpless.[3]

In 1902 he began a twelve-year period of prolific output. He wrote columns for the *Daily News* and the *Illustrated London News*, along with magazine articles for *The Speaker*, *The Clarion*, and *The Eye Witness*. In addition, he produced literary works of fiction: *The Napoleon of Notting Hill* (1904), *The Man Who Was Thursday* (1908), *The Ballad and the Cross* (1910), and,

[2] G. K. Chesterton, *The Autobiography of G. K. Chesterton*, in The Collected Works of G. K. Chesterton, vol. 16 (San Francisco: Ignatius Press, 1988), 21.

[3] Russell Sparkes, ed., *Prophet of Orthodoxy: The Wisdom of G. K. Chesterton* (London: HarperCollins, 1997), 23–24.

beginning in 1911, the Father Brown detective stories. There were works of literary criticism: *Robert Browning* (1903), *Charles Dickens* (1906), *George Bernard Shaw* (1909), and *The Victorian Age in Literature* (1912). What Russell Sparkes has described as the prophet in Chesterton began in 1903 with the articles in *The Clarion*. These were followed by such books as *Heretics* (1905), *Orthodoxy* (1908), and *What's Wrong with the World?* (1910). He also composed a major epic poem, *The Ballad of the White Horse*, in 1911.[4]

Chesterton was baptized in the Church of England, but he was not a practicing member. Rather, he had been raised in the fashion of a Unitarian, with no belief in the divinity of Christ or the doctrine of the Most Blessed Trinity. This vacuum was to take its toll, leading him into strange patterns of thinking and living. His thinking, by his own admission, became intellectual despair; his living, paganism. But God was not about to abandon this prophet of orthodoxy. Instead, two people, very crucial to Chesterton's future, were placed in his path. In 1896, he met Frances Blogg, the young Anglo-Catholic woman whom he would eventually marry and who would follow him into the Church. Four years later, he was introduced to the Catholic writer Hilaire Belloc, and they became fast friends.

There is little doubt that Frances Blogg and Hilaire Belloc moved Chesterton in the direction of Christian orthodoxy. This movement is best seen in his growing disenchantment with many ideological trends at the beginning of the twentieth century. He decided to write about those trends in 1905 in his book *Heretics*. Three years later, he followed with a work of truly monumental proportion, *Orthodoxy*:

[4] The chronological listing and dating appear exactly as in Sparkes, op. cit., 24.

> My first impulse to write, and almost my first impulse to think, was a revolt of disgust with the Decadents and the atheistic pessimism of the "nineties". . . . I thought that all the wit and wisdom of the world was banded together to slander and depress the world . . . then, above all, everyone claiming intelligence, insisted on "Art for art's sake". . . . I started to think it out, and the more I thought of it, the more certain I grew that the whole thing was a fallacy; that art could not exist from, still less in opposition to, life; especially the life of the soul which is salvation, and that great art never had been so much detached from conscience and common sense.[5]

And with that in mind, fourteen years before he converted to the Church of Rome, Chesterton produced his orthodox vision of the Christian church as expressed in the Apostles' Creed. *Orthodoxy* is a book extremely optimistic in tone. As Russell Sparkes has noted:

> Such positive convictions remained with G. K. C. for the rest of his life, and he became recognized as a great optimist, perhaps the only genuinely optimistic thinker our gloomy century has produced.[6]

That was 1908. In 1911, Chesterton's brother, Cecil, became a Roman Catholic, and his family, including G. K., was shocked. Cecil was not to have many years as a Catholic. His subsequent death and a nearly fatal illness for Gilbert caused the latter to take stock in his life and to seek counsel from friends, in particular, Monsignor Ronald Knox and Maurice Baring, both of whom had converted to Catholicism.

Eleven years separated Cecil and Gilbert Chesterton in their becoming Catholics. Long before 1922, however, ru-

[5] G. K. Chesterton, cited in Sparkes, op. cit., 20.
[6] Sparkes, op. cit., 10.

mors circulated that G. K. was seriously considering the Church of Rome. He was known to be a close friend of Father John O'Connor, a Catholic priest whom he and Frances had met in Yorkshire and a man who had helped Gilbert with serious inner struggles. That friendship provided Chesterton with the priest model for his first Father Brown detective story, "The Blue Cross". Being a spiritual novice of Father O'Connor further stimulated Gilbert to look into his own soul:

> It brought me in a manner face to face once more with those morbid but vivid problems of the soul . . . and gave me a great and growing sense that I had not found any spiritual solution of them. . . . That the Catholic Church knew more about good than I did was easy to believe. That she knew more about evil than I did, seemed incredible.[7]

He did not immediately act on this inner scrutiny. In fact, in 1915, when he was seriously ill and Father O'Connor paid a visit to his home in Beaconsfield, Frances would not allow the priest to see her husband. The time was not right, apparently, but it was in 1922, on Sunday, July 30. The site (in the absence of a Catholic church) was a small shed attached to the Railway Hotel in Beaconsfield. There Father O'Connor received Chesterton into the Church. In four years' time, his wife was to follow.

> Long afterwards I found what I meant stated much better by a Catholic writer: "God is not infinite; He is a synthesis of infinity and boundary!" . . . the other teachers were always men of one idea, even when their one idea was universality. . . . I have only found one creed that could not be satisfied with a truth, but only with the truth, which is made of a million such truths and yet is one.[8]

---

[7] Chesterton, cited in Sparkes, op. cit., 36–37.
[8] Ibid., 40.

That thought is from a marvelous little book G. K. wrote in 1926 called *The Catholic Church and Conversion*. Interest, indeed downright fascination, from so many parts of the world had accompanied his conversion that he wrote the book to shed light on the meaning of becoming a Catholic and, undoubtedly, to help others by illustrating more fully his own experience.

He began on a somewhat curious note, recalling that he had been raised free of strong anti-Catholic prejudice, not because the members of his family were devout and broad-minded, but rather because they were indifferent:

> [M]y family and friends were more concerned with the open-ing of the book of Darwin than the book of Daniel; and most of them regarded the Hebrew Scriptures as if they were Hittite sculptures.[9]

He nevertheless recognized the fact that many of the En-glish people had a great fear of Catholicism and, especially, a fear of those who were the most obvious representatives of it, the priests:

> Why should a man who wanted to be wicked encumber himself with special and elaborate promises to be good? There might sometimes be a reason for a priest being a profligate. But what was the reason for a profligate being a priest? There are many more lucrative walks of life in which a person with such shining talents for vice and villainy might have made a brighter use of his gifts. Why should a man encumber himself with vows that nobody could expect him to take and he did not himself expect to keep? Would any man make himself poor in order that he might become avaricious; or take a vow of chastity . . . in order to get into a little more trouble when he did not keep it? [10]

[9] G. K. Chesterton, *The Catholic Church and Conversion*, in The Collected Works of G. K. Chesterton, vol. 3 (San Francisco: Ignatius Press, 1990), 72.
[10] Ibid., 74.

Why, then, would people have such fears and prejudices about the Church? Chesterton took a guess at the answer:

> It must either mean that they suspect that our religion has something about it so wrong that the hint of it is bad for anybody; or else that it has something so right that the presence of it would convert anybody. To do them justice, I think most of them darkly suspect the second and not the first.[11]

Many of these same people who entertained such fears were also very quick to say that when a person converted to Catholicism he was entering a Church that forced him to believe certain truths. To them, G. K. had this reply:

> [I]t is not really a question of what a man is made to believe but of what he must believe; what he cannot help believing. He cannot disbelieve in an elephant when he has seen one; and he cannot treat the Church as a child when he has discovered that she is his mother. She is not only his mother, but his country's mother in being much older and more aboriginal than his country. She is such a mother not in sentimental feeling but in historical fact.[12]

Chesterton challenged the British nation a bit further when, alluding to the Book of Job in the Old Testament, where God says to the man, "Where were you when the foundations of the world were laid?", he imagined what a Catholic could say to England:

> "Where were you when the foundations of the Church were laid?" And the nation will not know in the least what to answer—if it should wish to answer—but will be forced to put its hand upon its mouth, if only like one who yawns and falls asleep.[13]

[11] Ibid.
[12] Ibid., 81.
[13] Ibid., 82.

In the story of most people's conversion to the Church, Chesterton saw a process of three steps:

1. The first phase is that of the young man who wishes to be objective about the Church, mostly because he sees so many who are not objective. G. K. drew a comparison with his own life when he worked for the *Daily News* of London. He once took the time to draw up a list of fifteen frequent misconceptions about the Catholic Church (with the intention of refuting them at some point).

2. The second phase is that in which the convert begins to be conscious not only of the misconceptions but of the delightful discovery of how much truth is to be found in the Church. Rather than as merely a second phase, Chesterton saw this step as measurable progress:

> This process . . . is perhaps the most pleasant and straightforward part of the business; easier than joining the Catholic Church and much easier than trying to live the Catholic life. It is like discovering a new continent full of strange flowers and fantastic animals, which is at once wild and hospitable.[14]

3. The third phase is when the convert comes painfully close to the truth: he has come so near the truth that he forgets it is "a magnet with the powers of attraction and repulsion". Chesterton describes with striking words what happens next:

> It is impossible to be just to the Catholic Church. The moment men cease to pull against it they feel a tug towards it. The moment they cease to shout it down they begin to listen to it with pleasure. The moment they try to be fair to it they begin to be fond of it. But when that affection has passed a certain point it begins to take on the tragic and menacing grandeur of a great love affair.[15]

[14] Ibid., 91.
[15] Ibid., 92.

Chesterton sums up his three phases this way:

> It is not the Pope who has set the trap or the priests who have
> baited it. The whole point of the position is that the trap is
> simply the truth. The whole point is that man himself has
> made his way towards the trap of truth, and not the trap that
> has run after the man.[16]

According to G. K., a Catholic convert most certainly did
not stop thinking; actually, the Church preserved that one
sure place where a person could begin to learn to think:

> The Catholic convert has for the first time a starting-point for
> straight and strenuous thinking. He has for the first time a
> way of testing the truth in any question that he raises.[17]

To be sure, Chesterton was a serious thinker prior to
entering the Church. But, as a Catholic, he proved this even
more. His friendly adversary, H. G. Wells, wrote a work
called *Outline of History*, which looked at world events from
an atheistic point of view. G. K. sought to refute this approach in a book written three years after his reception into
the Church: *The Everlasting Man*, a book enormously popular
in the nineteen-twenties and -thirties, was divided into two
parts. The first was an account of history leading up to the
Incarnation; the second, the life of Jesus Christ, the Everlasting Man. The book evoked this comment from Monsignor
Ronald Knox:

> If every other line he wrote should disappear from circula-
> tion, Catholic posterity would still owe him an immeasurable
> debt of gratitude so long as a copy of *The Everlasting Man*
> enriched its libraries.[18]

[16] Ibid.
[17] Ibid., 106.
[18] Ronald A. Knox, cited in Sparkes, op. cit., 81.

Another Chesterton masterpiece was written just three years before his death; it was his study of Saint Thomas Aquinas. Étienne Gilson, one of the great Thomistic philosophers of the twentieth century, had this to say about it:

> I consider it as being without possible comparison the best book ever written on St Thomas. Nothing short of genius can account for such an achievement. . . . [T]he few readers who have spent twenty or thirty years in studying St Thomas . . . cannot fail to perceive that the so-called 'wit' of Chesterton has put their scholarship to shame. He has guessed all that which they had tried to demonstrate, and he has said all that which they were more or less clumsily attempting to express in academic formulas.[19]

Through the course of Chesterton's Catholic life, in addition to his usual output of books and articles, he continually defended the Faith in print and gave regular lectures for the Catholic Evidence Guild. Since there was no Catholic church in Beaconsfield, the community where the Chestertons lived, G. K. and Frances helped to build one from their own resources.

In the spring of 1936, Chesterton became weaker and weaker. A visit to Lourdes was tried, but to no avail. It became obvious he was dying. His longtime secretary, Dorothy Collins, asked the newspapers not to bother his family, and it is a sign of the enormous respect in which he was held in Fleet Street that they complied.

In June 1936, the Dominican Father Vincent McNabb paid Chesterton the honor of singing over him the "Salve Regina", that great medieval hymn to our Lady, whom G. K. loved so dearly and that is sung over dying members of the Dominican order.

At Chesterton's death, Cardinal Eugenio Pacelli, the future

[19] Étienne Gilson, cited in Joseph Pearce, *Wisdom and Innocence: A Life of G. K. Chesterton* (San Francisco: Ignatius Press, 1996), 432.

Pope Pius XII, sent a telegram on behalf of Pope Pius XI to Cardinal Hinsley, archbishop of Westminster:

> Holy Father deeply grieved death Mr. Gilbert Keith Chesterton devoted son Holy Church gifted Defender of the Catholic Faith. His Holiness offers paternal sympathy people of England assures prayers dear departed, bestows Apostolic Benediction.[20]

Ronald Knox predicted that Chesterton would be remembered by Catholics as "a man who fought on the side of angels, a great model to the authors of all time of two virtues in particular—innocence and humility". His friend Hilaire Belloc, who considered him unparalleled in the world of English letters, said, "Chesterton will never occur again!" Maisie Ward considered him the "greatest man in the Catholic intellectual revival".[21]

Today, Beaconsfield is a brief, and very worthwhile, train ride from London. One can visit Top Meadow, the Chestertons' home, which is now maintained by the Saint Barnabas Society, formerly the Convert Aid Society of England; Saint Theresa's church, completed and beautified by contributions from G. K.'s friends and admirers around the world; and the graves of Gilbert and Frances Chesterton in the town cemetery.

In his life, G. K. proved the truth of words spoken by his friend Father Ronald Knox, words he applied directly to his own conversion:

> [T]he Catholic Church really does have to get on by hook or crook. That is, by the hook of the fisherman and the crook of the shepherd; and it is the hook that has to catch the convert and the crook that has to keep him.[22]

---

[20] Maisie Ward, *Gilbert Keith Chesterton* (New York: Sheed and Ward, 1943), 652.

[21] Morris, op. cit., 18–19.

[22] Chesterton, *Catholic Church and Conversion*, 122.

10

JACQUES MARITAIN

A genuine intellectual

The Basilica of Sacré Coeur in Paris is known throughout the world. It sits majestically atop the hill of Montmartre over-looking the city and has been a venerable landmark for de-cades. Far more important, it has been a center for perpetual adoration of our Lord in the Blessed Sacrament. In times past, it was very common to see hundreds of men and women spending entire nights in adoration of the Blessed Sacrament. Rich and poor, learned and unlearned, peasants and nobil-ity—all classes of society were united before the Body of Christ. One of those to be frequently found in deep prayer was a genuine intellectual and famous French convert, Jacques Maritain.

He was born in Paris, in 1882, into a family that did not provide him contact with organized religion. His father, Paul Maritain, was a Paris lawyer. He was neither hostile to reli-gion nor attracted to it. Maritain's mother, Geneviève Favre, was of quite a different background. Her father, Jules Favre, played an important role in the establishment of the Third French Republic, and, like so many of that political ilk, he considered that the supernatural had no role whatever in the affairs of state. Apparently, he passed these sentiments to his daughter.

I will be a socialist and live for the revolution. It is an enormous debt that I owe the proletariat. . . . [A]ll I can think and know I will devote to the proletariat and to humanity: I will use it entirely to prepare the revolution, to advance to some small degree the happiness and education of humanity.[1]

His parents bequeathed to Jacques a rationalist bias that, taken to its logical conclusion, gave him a strong feeling of the meaninglessness of life. His early education at the Lycée Henri IV merely added fuel to the flame. One bright spot occurred during these school years, however—his friendship with Ernest Psichari. The two were inseparable, and their approach to life was very similar. By the time they were matriculated in the Sorbonne, each had acquired a deep thirst for something that went beyond what mere science could prove. This search reached agonizing proportions; they were convinced the human situation had a deeper meaning.

Ernest Psichari was not the only student to share what one writer has called the "metaphysical anguish" of Maritain. Raïssa Oumansoff, the daughter of Russian Jewish immigrants, met Jacques early in their college careers. Jacques had been actively involved in a protest against the treatment of Russian socialist students at the Sorbonne, and she joined him in that protest. It was not long before the two were involved in many such causes, none of which provided ultimate satisfaction. Raïssa sought expression in poetry, and her future husband acquired a lifelong interest in it, due, no doubt, to her influence. As the couple grew closer, their intellectual difficulties became more pronounced. John Dunaway, a Maritain scholar, explains:

> The depth of metaphysical despair in which the young couple were brought together is attested to by a promise they made

[1] Geneviève Favre Maritain, cited in John M. Dunaway, *Jacques Maritain* (Boston: Twayne Publishers, 1978), 15.

to each other that if they failed to find the answer to the apparent meaninglessness of life within one year, they would both commit suicide. Predictably, this radical commitment to the quest for ultimate truth was ill received at the Sorbonne, but thanks to the suggestion of their Socialist friend Charles Péguy, the couple began to attend the public lectures that Henri Bergson was giving at the Collège de France.[2]

When Jacques and Raïssa were married in 1904, they had a certain tranquility of soul. Two very convincing French philosophers had proven to them the existence and attainability of objective truth. One year later, yet another Frenchman would take them a step further and, ultimately, into the Catholic Church.

"There is only one sadness in life," Léon Bloy once wrote, "not to be a saint." His life of poverty and asceticism was to bear this out, and he was to affect the Maritains deeply. Bloy's works have never been read as widely as they might have been, yet it was through his books that Jacques and Raïssa first met him. They contacted him for an appointment, and he readily agreed. He lived on the hill of Montmartre in Paris, and he was commonly referred to as the "thankless beggar". He had gathered about him a large circle of friends, impressed with the absolute sincerity of his style of life. Bloy once said, "I would give you all the artists in the world and all their masterpieces for one Our Father recited by a beggar, standing in a ditch." [3]

Crucial as this contact was, the Maritains would need a great deal of Bloy's advice before their difficulties were put to rest. Certain aspects of Christianity scandalized them, especially people who called themselves Christian but whose

[2] Dunaway, op. cit., 16.

[3] Rawley Myers, *Faith Experiences of Catholic Converts* (Huntington, Ind.: Our Sunday Visitor, 1992), 81.

personal lives fell far short of reflecting the gospel ethic. Raïssa, of a Jewish background, knew full well that her conversion to Catholicism would be viewed by her family as a betrayal of their heritage. In addition, being of a somewhat liberal nature politically, she initially saw no difficulty in accepting Church teaching without formally entering the Church. In this way, she would not have to be part of an ecclesial body that, she thought, associated itself too often with the forces of political reaction.

Such obstacles were overcome, but not without months of soul-searching. It is difficult to say if this was the first time in Jacques' life that he sincerely prayed, but, as a sense of near desperation overtook him, he petitioned that if God existed and if He were ultimate truth, His poor creature would be given light to grasp the truth. Raïssa was also overcome with prayer and found much solace in it. She had been seriously ill in the winter of 1906, and, during her convalescence, she and her husband had many conversations about the course they must pursue. On April 6, 1906, they told Léon Bloy they wished to be baptized in the Catholic Church. One can only guess at the joy he must have felt when these two "spiritual children" expressed their willingness to embrace the fullness of faith. Bloy referred them to Father Durantel, a priest at the Basilica of Sacré Coeur, for instruction.

Raïssa later noted that, during this time of study and waiting, both she and Jacques suffered periods of great uncertainty. Their problem was not one of grasping the truths of faith or intellectually accepting them; rather, they believed that in accepting Catholicism they would have to give up the life of the mind. They were exchanging philosophy for truth, but what they did not yet see was that, in that exchange, their philosophical interests would be enhanced and would serve to enhance the Body of Christ.

Jacques and Raïssa Maritain and Vera Oumansoff (Raïssa's sister, who had made her own intellectual journey to the Faith) were received into the Catholic Church on June 11, 1906, at the Church of Saint John the Evangelist on Montmartre. One year to the day after Léon Bloy had first received a letter from the Maritains, he had the great pleasure of serving as their godfather. They confided only to Bloy and one other close friend their peace and joy upon being baptized.

Family reaction brought no surprise. Raïssa's parents took it as a turning away from all she had ever been. Jacques' mother, Geneviève, was devastated. If anything, she would have wanted her son to follow the political path of his atheistic grandfather, Jules Favre, or the philosophical route of a later convert, Charles Péguy (whose early rejection of organized religion she so admired), or even Henri Bergson. He had let her down on all three counts. The Maritains suffered much and paid an enormous price for their conversion to Catholicism.

Perhaps feeling the need to distance themselves a bit, the Maritains moved to Germany, to the university town of Heidelberg, where Jacques studied experimental biology. He was already a philosopher by training, and, of the two disciplines, he felt a much stronger attraction to the latter. In 1905, he had received the *agrégé en philosophie*, which was sufficient qualification to teach on a graduate level and more than sufficient for a secondary level. When the couple returned to France in 1908, they had been Catholics two years, and their fervency was particularly strong. Jacques was anxious to teach philosophy, but a philosophy that was strongly rooted in the truths of Catholicism, not philosophy that a particular faculty might require him to teach.

Back in Paris, they met Father Humbert, a Dominican

priest, who became their mentor. Because Raïssa had a pre-
carious state of health and was often confined at home, the
priest suggested she start to read the *Summa theologia* of Saint
Thomas Aquinas. It transformed her, and she became an
enormous influence on her husband. In Jacques, Thomism
was a seed planted in very fertile soil. He was ready to "drink
in" all that Aquinas had to offer: "It was as much a conversion experience as meeting Bloy had been, a joyous flood
or enlightenment, and the definitive revelation of his life's
vocation." [4]

In 1912, Jacques began teaching at the Collège Stanislas, a
Catholic secondary school in Paris. His was not the secular
strain of thought found in many of the nation's schools.
Indeed, even though the college was under Catholic auspices,
many considered it quite unusual when Jacques announced
he would begin his classes by praying the Ave Maria. The
following year, he began lecturing at the Institute Catholique,
which provided him an even greater opportunity to teach
Thomistic philosophy. As John Dunaway has said: "[T]he
audience was witnessing the first public manifesto of the
Catholic Renaissance, one of the great cultural movements of
the first half of our century." [5]

The Maritains had been left a generous amount of money
from a friend, and with it they purchased a home that they
converted into a center for the study of Thomism. Located
at Meudon, a suburb between Paris and Versailles, it provided
a locale where scholars could gather for the exchange of
ideas. This delighted Jacques. The logical nature of Thomistic
thought was a contagious attraction to those who came to
Meudon, not to mention the fact that in Thomism they
found answers, not simply the creation of questions with no

[4] Dunaway, op. cit., 18.
[5] Ibid., 19.

answers. The view has been expressed by many scholars that Maritain's most significant contribution as a philosopher was his adaptation of Thomism to modern thought, much as Thomas had adapted Aristotle to Christian thought.

The Maritains were not living in France when the Nazis invaded it. Jacques was lecturing at the Pontifical Institute of Mediæval Studies in Toronto. His political views were well known. His wife's religious background was equally known. The so-called Free French were supporters of the exiled government of Charles de Gaulle, and Jacques and Raïssa were among their number. Jacques often spoke on "Voice of America" radio, advancing the cause of French liberation. He did the same in 1941 in a well-circulated book, *France, My Country through the Disaster.*

Maritain never ceased being a philosopher, but at specific moments in his career his emphasis varied. During the war years, he seemed to emphasize more practical topics. *Education at the Crossroads*, in 1943, had a decidedly humanistic tone. In the same year, *Christianity and Democracy* might be said to echo the principles of America's founding fathers, at least in their insistence that true democracy has its ultimate origin in God. That, to Maritain, was one of America's great strengths. He lived in the United States in the forties and fifties and wrote his impressions in a 1958 work, *Reflections on America.*

Charles de Gaulle became president of France at the war's end, and shortly after he requested Maritain to accept the position of French ambassador to the Holy See. The social nature of such an appointment interested neither Jacques nor Raïssa, but their devotion to Church and country compelled them to accept. From 1945 to 1948, Vatican City was their home. While ambassador, Jacques was much involved with the worker-priest movement. A number of French clerics, wishing to show their solidarity with poor factory workers, joined them in the work force, hoping to bring the workers closer to the Church. Maritain supported the movement in principle but was unable to convince Vatican officials of its effectiveness. The movement was suppressed in the forties, only to be allowed some two decades later.

One of the more significant friendships Maritain formed in these years was with Giovanni Montini, the future Pope Paul VI. The details, as given in this 1978 account, are especially interesting:

> The Vatican official was so profoundly influenced by the French philosopher that he has since called himself a disciple of Maritain and has even footnoted him in the encyclical *Populorum Progressio* ("On the Development of Peoples"). Perhaps the greatest honor of Jacques Maritain's career came when Pope Paul, at the end of Vatican II, addressed a message to intellectuals of the world through Maritain and publicly embraced him in Saint Peter's Square.[6]

When Maritain's term as ambassador concluded, many thought he would return to France. The war had changed much in his homeland, however, and he doubted the extent of his influence there. Instead, he accepted a teaching offer from Harold Dodd, president of Princeton University. His years in New Jersey afforded him opportunity to write on many topics. In 1952 he gave the Mellon Lectures on the fine arts in Washington, D.C., later published as *Creative Intuition in Art and Poetry*. This was followed by *Man and the State*, *The Responsibility of the Artist*, and *On the Philosophy of History*. At heart, though, Maritain was always a Thomist, and it is interesting to observe how at least one commentator viewed Maritain's impact on Thomism in America:

[6] Ibid., 23.

Within the Catholic community itself, Maritain's presence in America has made more concrete and feasible the ideal of a Christian layman devoting himself entirely to the work of philosophy, whether as a Thomist or not. Maritain's fidelity to that vocation has encouraged laymen to devote their scholarly energy to work in the field of philosophy. It has also helped them to see that one can engage in rigorous and fruitful philosophical studies precisely as a Christian thinker who is also responsive to the influence of his faith.[7]

A topic that occupied much of Maritain's life was the Jewish question, specifically, anti-Semitism. He wrote very forcefully and did not hesitate to describe it as a sin against God's people. He wrote, however, from a Christian perspective, and many Jewish commentators felt he could not adequately grasp the devastating nature of such bigotry. From a Catholic point of view, his contribution was substantial. Michael Novak explains:

> [T]he debt Catholics owe to Jacques Maritain for his reflections on Judaism is enormous. As teacher to a whole generation of Bishops and theologians, his contribution to the statement of Vatican II on the Jews was significant, perhaps philosophically indispensable. Maritain saw that the validity of the Jewish vocation under God is forever; that God's covenant with the Jews is unbreakable; and that the friendship between Christians and Jews is an obligation springing directly from the vocation of both as vessels of God's inscrutable love.[8]

Maritain lost his beloved Raïssa in 1960, and he returned to

---

[7] James Collins, "Maritain's Impact on Thomism in America", in Joseph W. Evans, ed., *Jacques Maritain: The Man and His Achievement* (New York: Sheed and Ward, 1963), 27.

[8] Michael Novak, "Maritain and the Jews", in Robert Royal, *Jacques Maritain and the Jews* (South Bend, Ind.: University of Notre Dame Press, 1994), 128–29.

France the following year. Her sister Vera had preceded her in death, and Jacques was left quite alone. A religious order in Toulouse called the Little Brothers of Jesus, whose rule was based on the life of Father Charles de Foucauld, welcomed him into their community. There he remained until his death in April 1973, at age ninety-one. His life was far from idle. He edited *Raïssa's Journal*, wrote *On the Church of Christ*, and produced a work called *The Peasant of the Garonne*, which many considered a reversal of positions he had espoused for years. The Second Vatican Council had sanctioned much of Maritain's thought, but, at the end of his life, he may well have been rebelling against perceived abuses of that same Council. Throughout his life, Maritain believed God wanted him to use his intelligence as a "subtly flashing sword in the defense of faith", and from that belief he never wavered.

11

KARL STERN

From Old Testament to New

The Russian novelist Dostoyevsky once said that the divinity of Christ "is the one question on which everything in the world depends".[1] That statement formed the very foundation of the conversion of Karl Stern, a Bavarian-born psychiatrist who told the world his story some decades ago in an inspiring book *The Pillar of Fire*. Karl Stern found it very difficult to put the innermost feelings of his heart into words. Christ's stirring an individual soul is very personal, yet, given that limitation, he wanted to tell people, to the best of his ability, what had brought him to the Catholic Church. Stern was a German Jew who grew up in a small town, one of the oldest in Bavaria. Several rabbis were to be found in earlier generations of his family, and most of the Jews with whom he was raised made their livelihood in either the retail or wholesale market. Karl grew up with his parents, his grandfather, and his brother Ludwig, some ten years younger. His parents had no familiarity with Hebrew, but his grandfather had once studied to be a rabbi. He did not finish his course, but he had sufficient knowledge to conduct synagogue services:

> My grandfather was the only one in our congregation who had received Jewish instruction. He was, for instance, the

[1] Karl Stern, *The Pillar of Fire* (New York: Harcourt, Brace, 1951), 4.

only one besides the Cantor who knew the liturgy well enough to conduct part of the service during the holidays. For as long as I could remember, he had been the president of the congregation, which consisted of about twenty families. . . . Yet he was not at all orthodox, and assumed the somewhat lax attitude of compromise frequent with Western Jews. For example, he kept his store open on Saturdays, and took it for granted that his children did not keep the Mosaic dietary laws. On the other hand, he never missed a service except during sickness. He participated in three Sabbath services, those on Monday and Thursday mornings, many annual memorial services for the dead and, since there were things such as semi-holidays, it happened not infrequently that he went to the synagogue seven times a week.[2]

Curiously, some of his earliest education was Catholic. Stern attended the town's only kindergarten, one conducted by Catholic sisters. Mrs. Stern had been the first Jewish woman in the community to send her child there, and Karl had his earliest exposure to Christianity listening to New Testament stories and reciting brief prayers. Years later, he recalled the piety of the place and how that must have impressed him.

At age ten, he was sent to boarding school in a neighboring town, and a year later he continued his studies in Munich, where he boarded with an Orthodox Jewish family and had his first real taste of strict Jewish Orthodoxy. The Orthodox synagogue made a deep impression on him:

Many prayed for themselves without paying attention to their neighbors, often without reference to what the Cantor was doing. Many closed their eyes in devotion and made characteristic rhythmic movements forward and backward. This diminished the danger of distraction. Everybody seemed to

[2] Ibid., 12.

know the liturgy by heart and followed the reading of Torah and Prophet with the most amazing knowledge of detail. Anyone from the congregation might be called upon to read from the Prophets.[3]

What is even more interesting is the way Stern, thinking of an old rabbi who was very formal but full of goodness and wisdom, drew a connection between one religion's tradition and another:

> Somewhere underneath this seemingly impenetrable crust of formalism, the essence is buried; there you find . . . words such as "Love Thy Neighbor as Thyself," words which are seldom expressed, as if out of some pious diffidence. . . . The interesting thing is that in Christian orthodoxy, too, the on- looker often sees nothing but empty formalism behind which one cannot see the "Christian ideas" any more. Here, too, the Catholic Church represents the most direct development from Jewish orthodox tradition.[4]

It began to bother Stern that the children around him knew Hebrew very well. Writing decades later, he specifically mentions his lack of knowledge of the significance of the Day of Atonement and the sacrifice of the scapegoat. To him, the books of Isaiah and Jonah were little more than titles. There were specific prayers of contrition recited by Jews, but, again, his background was only rudimentary. With all these defi- ciencies, one would think the experience of Orthodox Juda- ism would have had little impact on him. In fact, the opposite happened; this religious exposure penetrated deeply and had lasting effect.

In the years following the First World War, there was what Stern describes as a "profound spiritual restlessness" in much

[3] Ibid., 37.
[4] Ibid., 38.

of Europe. This was stronger, he felt, in Germany than in the British Isles. The later twentieth century described it as a generation gap, and it affected the Jewish community seriously. Younger Jews in Germany, Poland, and Russia were strongly attracted to Zionism and envisioned a future life in Palestine. Karl Stern joined an association of young Jews and became quite active. He formed many friendships, but, as one commentator has noted, he was "thrown in with many doubtful youths".[5]

Christian pacifism is far removed from Zionist ideals, so it is surprising that the young Jewish students were receptive to it, but the writings of Frederich Wilhelm Foerster, a strong opponent of any type of postwar rearmament, attracted Karl Stern and his friends. It was the writer's emphasis on sacrifice, self-denial, and personal heroism that was most compelling. Because of his views, Foerster came under sharp criticism from militant right-wing political groups in Germany. Prudent it was, in retrospect, for the Bavarian government to appoint him minister to Switzerland. Stern noted about Foerster: "Although he was not a Catholic, he was in the habit of quoting such writers as Saint Catherine of Siena and Saint Teresa of Avila." [6]

Karl's years in medical school would take him to Munich, Berlin, and Frankfurt. During this time, he met a Jewish psychiatrist, Ernest Haase, who ran a free clinic for drug addicts and alcoholics. The work seemed to Karl a way of helping the neediest of the needy. He quickly joined Dr. Haase and apparently found great satisfaction in rehabilitative therapy. Medical school completed, Karl followed Haase's lead in another area. He began studies at the Institute for

[5] Rawley Myers, *Faith Experiences of Catholic Converts* (Huntington, Ind.: Our Sunday Visitor, 1992), 51.

[6] Stern, op. cit., 57.

Psychiatry in Munich and eventually joined the staff. By then Hitler had come to power in Germany and had begun to speak of racial superiority in the most militant way. It was amazing to Karl Stern that so many people, often very good, sincere people, unthinkingly joined the Nazi Party. Once the intense persecution of the Jews started, the atmosphere at the Institute became very tense. Being a Jew, Stern was especially apprehensive, though his colleagues assured him they would do everything in their power to protect him. All was not fear, however. At the Institute, certain people with whom he was closely involved in medical research had significant impact on his future. The Yamagiwas were a Japanese couple somewhat ignored by their Japanese co-workers because they professed a Christian creed. Frau Flamm, a lab technologist, was a fervent Catholic and daily communicant. What was it about Christianity that commanded such loyalty? One could almost hear Karl Stern's ever-searching soul asking the question.

He visited his hometown and spoke of how things were different—everyone nervous, tense, anxious, fearful:

> It was a great paradox that one of the vilest and most cruel racial persecutions in history hit a people which was amazingly well integrated into the cultural life of its "host." For the German Jews, as is well known, were the most assimilated and most deeply rooted Jews in Europe, perhaps with the exception of the Italian ones.[7]

How, then, make any sense out of events?

> [T]he drama in history which I have witnessed myself, the fate of European Jewry, was either meaningless, or else its meaning was transcendental. There is no other alternative. Now if you believe in the existence of God the first possibility is excluded, and that agony of horror which we have

[7] Ibid., 155.

witnessed in our time must have a meaning which transcends all materialist dialectics. Since I believed in the existence of God, the answer was obvious.[8]

Taking his thoughts a step further, Stern had to ask if what was going on around him had any hidden meaning. Where was he to look for it? He began by turning to the Old Testament prophets, who, he believed, spoke to men and women of every age. The prophets spoke of grandeur and power, which seemed to be matched by the political and social thoughts and programs of the current regime. Then, too, Karl became increasingly aware of the evolution in his own thought:

> I must admit that in the beginning I, like many of us, had a somewhat childlike and simple idea. . . . I thought that these catastrophes in Jewish history happen as a punishment, and that the terrible persecution had befallen us because most of us had forgotten that we were Jews and had abandoned the ways of God laid down in the law. This is a rather simpli-fied . . . version of the prophetic concept of history. Its absur-dity becomes obvious when you consider events in the light of individual cases. My own grandmother, . . .who lived an exceptionally saintly life, died at the age of eighty-six in a concentration camp. What was she "punished" for?[9]

As Stern's search continued, God's revelation through the Old Testament prophets took on increased importance. From this, he came to a deeper appreciation of a personal Messiah, as that concept was understood in Judaism. It had become vague in much Jewish thinking, and that may have accounted for the impact of a hypothetical question put to Karl Stern about whether Jesus might be the longed-for Messiah. The

[8] Ibid., 163.
[9] Ibid., 164–65.

questioner meant little. The man of whom he asked the question could not stop thinking about it.

In 1933, His Eminence Cardinal Faulhaber was preaching a series of Advent sermons in his cathedral in Munich. One of the sermons was titled "Jewry and Christianity". What attracted Stern to go into the cathedral that evening? The title, perhaps, along with the influences that had molded his life up to that point and the current stirrings of his emotions. In any event, he listened carefully to the cardinal as he spoke of the unity of Jews and Christians and of Christianity's roots in Judaism. God's grace came to Karl that evening. A certitude began to grow that Christianity was the fulfillment of all that the prophets had taught:

> The sermon came as if it had been specially timed and written for my personal consumption. It had a profound, irrevocable influence on me. I remember well that, with the few meager hints he gave of the Paulinian idea with regard to post-Christian Judaism, he opened up an entirely new vista. I felt like a child who had known its own house from inside and from the garden, and who is now, for the first time, shown it from far away as part of the landscape.[10]

His Jewish belief in "election" seemed seriously threatened, and he was caught up in great inner turmoil and confusion; there seemed to be more to it than the view that Christianity and Islam were the two sister offshoots of the ancient religion.

Two difficulties had to be resolved. First, the Jews and the Nazis both guarded very carefully their "racial wall around the God of Sinai". Second, Jesus Christ did not come into the world to found a specifically unique branch of Judaism. Rather, he came to the Jewish people with his claim to be

[10] Ibid., 171.

Lord and Messiah. Of the two difficulties, the second would have to be answered with a total commitment of mind and heart. Stern was able to accept the messiahship of Christ but not his divinity. He thought a visit to the Jewish theologian Martin Buber would enhance his knowledge. It did, but the ultimate act of faith would have to be Karl Stern's.

> I had proudly re-stated, at least before myself, the absolute reality of the things of the spirit. The bold and defiant cry of the seventeenth-century mathematician, Pascal, that God is "not the God of Philosophers, but the God of Abraham, Isaak, and Jacob" had become my own. And now, not long after the beginning of my journey, I was facing the eternal question: "And who do you say that I am?" [11]

The light at the end of the tunnel eventually came. Karl's career brought him to England, to work at the Medical Research Council, a neurological center in London. While there, he met and married Liselotte. He also had his first serious encounter with the thought of Thomas Aquinas, specifically that saint's writings on the virtue of hope. These writings were far superior to anything he had encountered in natural psychology.

> I used to sit on a bench on Primrose Hill and look over all the City of London. If it were true, I used to think, that God had become man, and that His life and death had a personal meaning to every single person among all those millions of existences spent in the stench of slums, in a horizonless world, in the suffocating anguish of enmities, sickness and dying—if that were true, it would be something tremendously worth living for. [12]

---

[11] Ibid., 173.
[12] Ibid., 229.

For the first time in his life he went into a Catholic church to pray, the church of the Dominican Fathers in Hempstead, near where the Sterns were living. He went there every morning before work; it was all very unfamiliar to him, but prayer seemed to flow spontaneously from his heart.

In June 1939, Karl Stern, his wife, and their little boy (then one year old) left London for Montreal, Canada, where he had obtained a position on the staff of a mental hospital on the outskirts of the city. His thoughts shortly after his arrival in Canada are significant:

> For quite some time I thought that it was possible to remain a Jew and yet guard the secret of Jesus. I know that there are many who remain in this peculiar state. There are some very outstanding examples—Henri Bergson, Franz Werfel, Sholem Asch. It was impossible that, at this moment when our people was undergoing its agony, even Christ Himself would demand of one of us to become a deserter.[13]

With each passing year, Stern's spiritual journey was leading him into a prayerful study of the New Testament. In addition, he was reading Aquinas, Augustine, the *Pensées* of Pascal, and the works of the convert John Henry Cardinal Newman. He felt a great closeness with much of their thought, and he believed many other Jews would also. Karl had become very close to one of the nuns of the Sacred Heart who had a convent near the Sterns' home. He confided his admiration for these authors to her but admitted a glaring difficulty. Christianity as he conceived it in his mind differed greatly from daily experience: "As long as this incongruity existed, it seemed almost to be the mysterious task of the Jews to keep out." [14]

[13] Ibid., 246.
[14] Ibid., 247.

Two very significant people were now to come into the life of Karl and Liselotte Stern, and they would have a decisive influence on their further development; one was Jacques Maritain;, the other was Dorothy Day—both converts, both "spiritual mentors" to would-be converts.

Karl had had a longstanding desire to meet Maritain, because he believed no one else in the Church had such a tremendous grasp of the Jewish question. He told Maritain his reason for wanting to convert might be less than honest, namely, a desire to escape the fate of Jewry. Maritain implored him to put such self-analysis aside and to concentrate on the spiritual insight given him by God's grace, something that goes far beyond psychological probing.

> He spoke of the bleeding wounds on the visible body of the Church; of the divinity of Christ as a stumbling block for the Jews. He spoke in a peculiarly sketchy way, in hints rather than statements. Yet there was an impression of substance and clarity about everything he said.[15]

On Whitsunday 1954, Liselotte Stern and the two elder Stern children were received into the Catholic Church by Father Couturier, a French Dominican, a friend of Matisse and Picasso, with whom the Sterns also were friends.

> Even then I doubted my moral right to leave the Jewish community by a visible sign. The issues of supernatural and natural charity, of natural and supernatural justice, of loyalty and of treason seemed so hopelessly entangled that I continued in a state of bewildered search.[16]

In Dorothy Day, Stern had found many of the same qualities he admired in Maritain, especially an inner peace and tranquility that underlay the certitude of the convert's faith

---

[15] Ibid., 251–52.
[16] Ibid., 256.

decision. There seemed one difficulty to be overcome. What about anti-Semitism in the Catholic Church? Would it be too uncomfortable an atmosphere once he had joined?

> The Jew who has perceived Christ in the Church enters it not *in spite of* the fact that many of its members harbor an ignorant and prejudiced hatred against his people, but *because* of this fact. Here for the first time he is facing the demand of the Gospel in its terrible actuality.[17]

In the autumn of 1943, ten years after he had sat in the cathedral of Munich and listened to Cardinal Faulhaber, Karl Stern approached Father Ethelbert, an elderly Franciscan priest in Montreal, and asked to be received into the Catholic Church. He, in turn, referred Karl to Miss Sharp. Blind, elderly, and herself a convert, Miss Sharp made her home at the convent of the Grey Nuns in Montreal and was actively engaged in the apostolate of instruction. On the vigil of the Feast of Saint Thomas the Apostle, December 21, 1943, Father Ethelbert received Karl Stern into the Catholic Church. The next day, December 22, he made his First Communion. It was only after his reception of the sacrament that he read the Gospel for the Feast, the story of Thomas' refusal to believe until he had seen the wounds of Christ.

Karl Stern had not seen, but he had believed!

---

[17] Ibid., 263.

12

BRITISH AND FRENCH
LITERARY CONVERTS

Maurice Baring

There is a painting in the National Portrait Gallery in London of G. K. Chesterton, Hilaire Belloc, and Maurice Baring. Of the three, Baring's name is likely the least recognizable. His story of conversion, however, is one that bears telling.

Maurice Baring was born into a well-to-do family, the eighth son of Lord Revelstoke. His earliest years were spent in Berkeley Square, London, and his summers at Coombe Cottage, far from the bustle of the city. His education was taken at Eton and Cambridge. At Eton, he became friendly with Arthur Benson (the brother of Monsignor Robert Hugh Benson), who introduced him to his lifelong interest in Russian literature. At Cambridge, he passed a competitive exam for the diplomatic service, which he seemed to want to make his life's work.

Upon his university graduation in 1898, he became attaché to the British embassy in Paris, and he rose rather quickly to third secretary. He was not there one full year when he published his first book, written entirely in French, a language he had thoroughly mastered. From Paris he was sent to the British embassy in Rome in 1901. In the words of one of his biographers, the city's beauty "pierced him like an arrow".[1]

During these years spent working for the foreign service, Baring managed a trip to Russia, which he enjoyed so much he vowed to return. He was able to secure a six-month leave of absence for visits to Saint Petersburg and Moscow in 1903, and when the Russo-Japanese War broke out, he was hired as a military correspondent by the *London Morning Post*. He remained in Russia until 1907, when he returned to a literary and journalistic career in London.

Maurice Baring became a Catholic on February 1, 1909. He was never inclined to speak freely about his conversion, nor did he speak about his religious background, which could generally be termed Protestant, though lacking any serious denominational ties. As a young boy traveling in France he had made the acquaintance of an elderly curé, with whom he maintained social contact through the years. Then, while working for the foreign service, an interesting episode occurred:

> [I]n 1899 he went to Paris, and attended a low Mass in the Church of Our Lady of Victories, and it seemed to stun him. He had linked up the Catholic liturgy, in his mind, with a scandalously ostentatious pageantry: yet here he met with a silence more complete, more thrilling, than that of Nature herself. Moreover, the attitude of the worshippers filled him with amazement.[2]

Probably the best insight into Baring's conversion is provided by his 1925 novel *Cat's Cradle*. In this work, in a Roman setting, there is a dialogue between two non-Catholic English princesses, Blanche and Roccapalumba. The latter belonged to the Roman aristocracy, though she had been born in

---

[1] Raymond Las Vergnas, *Chesterton, Belloc, Baring* (New York: Sheed and Ward, 1938), 93.

[2] Ibid, 115.

England. A great deal of personal distress had attracted her to Catholicism as a possible solution to her difficulties. She confides to Blanche a thought she once heard expressed: "Catholic priests are so much more human than our clergymen; they study human nature and they are trained to understand people and to allow for the weaknesses and vanity of human nature."

Blanche listens to her friend Roccapalumba, but her own mind is more attracted to an argument from reason: "If the Roman Dogmas are false, what about the Protestant ones— for these derive from those? And if the spell of Rome were but trustworthy, what a difference that would make!"

Blanche returns to England, enters a Catholic church in her native village, assists at low Mass, and leaves with a feeling she had never experienced in Anglicanism: "She was possessed by the impression of truth; of fidelity to ultimate origins, that was breathed forth from the humble tabernacle." [3]

The narrator then describes a conversation that ensues between an unknown person and a Catholic priest, to which Blanche is privy. The priest asks if the person with whom he is speaking is Catholic. "No, but I'm Christian", came the reply. At some point, known to God, Blanche realizes that this same Christianity finds its completeness and fulfillment in Catholicism. "After her First Communion, [she] understood that the difference was not of degree, but of kind." [4]

The novel has Blanche being received into the Catholic Church in London's famed Brompton Oratory. After ten years of his own struggle and uncertainty, Maurice Baring, by then a well-known British novelist, was received into the Church in that same Oratory.

<hr/>

[3] Maurice Baring, quoted in Las Vergnas, op. cit., 116–17.
[4] Ibid., 117–18.

Sir Arnold Lunn

The question of imperfect leaders, the Inquisition, slavery, belief in eternal punishment, indulgences, the problem of biblical interpretation: such are the difficulties Arnold Lunn wrestled with prior to his conversion. He discussed them all, in the years after he became a Catholic, with his close friend William F. Buckley, Jr. Buckley, the esteemed founder of *National Review*, wrote an autobiography, *Nearer, My God*, in which he spends nearly forty pages summarizing conversations he and Sir Arnold had over the years and the particulars of belief each man analyzed.[5] In 1933, when he became a Catholic, Arnold Lunn was forty-five years of age, and he had already had a distinguished career.

He was born in 1888 in Madras, India. His father, an Englishman, and his mother, an Irish Protestant, provided his religious background, a combination of Anglicanism and Methodism. He attended Harrow and later Oxford, but in his student days he seems to have displayed a keener interest in sports, specifically mountain climbing and skiing, than in his studies.

This is not to suggest scholastic ability was lacking. Far from it. In fact, certain reading in college caused him to lose his faith. He chose journalism early in life, and he was known to be critical and cynical in his writing. Proof of this cynicism is *The Harrovians*, a book he wrote offering an unusual look at his alma mater and its traditions. This was followed by *Roman Converts*, in which he considers five individuals and their reasons for "Poping". At the book's outset, Lunn states that Catholicism has "caused more un-

<hr>

[5] William F. Buckley, Jr., *Nearer, My God: An Autobiography of Faith* (New York: Doubleday, 1997), 52–90.

merited suffering than any other institution in the history of the world".[6]

The Church, he suggested, seemed to rob its members of the right to use their minds, to engage in any intellectual pursuits; why in heaven's name would anyone want to join it? G. K. Chesterton became a Catholic simply because he enjoyed acting in a fashion contrary to what was expected; Monsignor Ronald Knox took delight in being fascinating. But Lunn seemed to be protesting just a bit too much. He went on to write a biography of John Wesley, founder of Methodism, and then *The Flight from Reason*, which sounded considerably less anti-Catholic. In the early thirties, Lunn became involved in two controversies, one with Monsignor Ronald Knox, the other with an agnostic named C. E. M. Joad. Put quite simply, he found Knox' arguments far more convincing than his own. Evelyn Waugh, a biographer of Monsignor Knox, notes that "Sir Arnold was received into the Church by Ronald in July 1933, less than two years after the last letter was put in the post, and became the most tireless Catholic apologist of his generation."[7]

This is very true. Lunn became a great booster of, and contributor to, the Catholic Intellectual Revival, both in England and the United States. He was a great friend of Frank Sheed (of Sheed and Ward), and once the two of them engaged in a debate at Hunter College in New York. In his memoir *The Church and I*, Sheed writes that, by mutual agreement, each took the side that did not represent his thinking. Sheed, who was born and raised a Catholic, took the position that converts had provided at least eighty percent of the literature of the Catholic Intellectual Revival. Arnold Lunn, a convert, was supposed to argue that cradle Catholics had

[6] Arnold Lunn, *Roman Converts* (New York: Scribner's, 1925), 11.
[7] Evelyn Waugh, *Monsignor Ronald Knox* (Boston: Little, Brown, 1959), 236.

contributed just as substantially, if not more. When it came
time to give his argument, however, he stood up but could
hardly think of any contributions cradle Catholics had
made.[8]

Between 1936 and 1939, Arnold taught a semester each
year at the University of Notre Dame. He was not overly
impressed with the intellectual quality of many students, noting that sports, for many, ranked higher than academics:

> We should aim at producing a team of Notre Dame debaters
> on fundamental religious issues which would be as formidable
> and as famous as the Notre Dame football team.[9]

In a sense, he was trying to make Catholic apologists out of
Notre Dame alumni; they would have to learn every possible
argument against their Faith in order to refute it. Arnold did
not stop with religion. He considered that dangerous political
movements had to be combated with equal fervency. Communism, "the final form of the service state",[10] was his specific target. If Catholic graduates held fast in both areas, the
world would be holier and safer.

Lunn died in 1974, at the age of eighty-six, at his home in
Switzerland.

Evelyn Waugh and Graham Greene

Evelyn Waugh and Graham Greene both converted to Catholicism in their mid-twenties. The experience affected
each man in a different way, but the uniqueness of the

---

[8] Frank Sheed, *The Church and I* (Garden City: Doubleday, 1974), 109.

[9] Arnold Lunn, cited in Patrick Allitt, *Catholic Converts: British and American
Intellectuals Turn to Rome* (Ithaca: Cornell University Press, 1997), 202.

[10] Arnold Lunn, *Spanish Rehearsal* (New York: Sheed and Ward, 1937), vii.

experience was a theme brilliantly woven into their novels. Their educational backgrounds were similar: Church of England prep schools and Oxford University. Their lives were also parallel in the military service they rendered their country during the Second World War. Graham Greene was assigned to West Africa, while Evelyn Waugh went to Yugoslavia. Randolph Churchill, the prime minister's son, specifically requested Evelyn to be part of a British Force aiding the Catholic Croatians in their struggle against Tito's Communist regime. The experience, his biographer noted, left him "deeply disillusioned".[11]

Waugh's conversion was not emotional, it was well reasoned. The son of a London publisher, he had both a family and an educational background that taught him to think. He was received into the Church in 1930 at Farm Street, the landmark Jesuit residence near Grosvenor Square, by Father Martin Cyril D'Arcy, an equally famous English Jesuit who claimed, during the course of Waugh's instruction, never to have had an unintellectual conversation with his student.

Fifteen years after his conversion, Waugh wrote *Brideshead Revisited*:

> Not since the time of Robert Hugh Benson . . . over thirty years before, had novelists of high ambition taken Christian religion as the main subject of a fiction to be treated without skepticism. . . . Evelyn was doing something which seemed in England to have gone out of fashion forever. He was making religion the central point of a story about contemporary English life, and approaching his theme with respect and awe.[12]

After *Brideshead Revisited*, he wrote a trilogy, *Sword of Honor*,

[11] Christopher Sykes, *Evelyn Waugh: A Biography* (Boston: Little, Brown, and Company, 1975), 202.

[12] Ibid., 248–49.

that portrayed the devastating effects of the Second World War through Catholic eyes.

Graham Greene, Waugh's contemporary, grew up in the suburbs of London, the son of the headmaster of Berkhamstead School. As an Oxford undergraduate, he was given to periods of severe melancholy, and he became addicted to playing Russian roulette. He edited a newspaper for some years in the Midlands, where he met his wife-to-be, Vivien Dayrell-Browning, who was instrumental in his conversion. Equally important was one Father Trollope, who instructed him in the Faith and received him into the Church. In his autobiography, *A Sort of Life*, Green admits his first impression of the priest was anything but favorable:

> At the first sight he was all I detested in my most private image of the Church. A very tall and a very fat man with big smooth jowls which looked as though they had never needed a razor, he resembled closely a character in one of those nineteenth century paintings to be seen in art shops on the wrong side of Piccadilly—monks and cardinals enjoying their Friday abstinence by dismembering enormous lobsters and pouring great goblets of wine.[13]

That did not remain his lifelong impression. As he came to know Father Trollope, he became increasingly impressed with the good he found in the man and even more with the unusually persuasive manner in which he presented the great truths of the Faith. Greene's conversion, unlike Waugh's, was not an intellectual one. It was not by strong philosophical arguments that he came to the Church, but by faith in God's existence and through the sincerity of the priest who helped him grow in the knowledge of God.

[13] Graham Greene, *A Sort of Life* (New York: Simon and Schuster, 1971), 165.

Much as Waugh had done in *Brideshead*, Greene did in 1938 with his first major religious novel, *Brighton Rock*. This story about the nature of evil contains many events whose surface meaning invites one to look deeper and discover penetrating Catholic truths.

It is curious that both men, much as they admired the Catholic ideal in their writings, fell short of it in the reality of broken marriages. Of the two, Waugh was firmer in his commitment. He also differed from Greene in the route his literary career took. In later years he wrote a well-received biography of Monsignor Ronald Knox, a convert who paid a great price for becoming a Catholic.

Waugh also wrote a biography of the sixteenth-century Jesuit martyr Edmund Campion, and he gave his author royalties to the Jesuits' famous Campion Hall at Oxford. There were several who felt that Waugh should not concern himself with such a topic, depressing in many of its details and possibly opening old wounds. The critics felt it would not be well received. Frank Sheed summed up such thinking:

> One critic begged him [Waugh], almost with tears in his eyes, not to let himself in for something that would be just about as cheerful as a wet Sunday afternoon in Manchester [England]. But the book was written. Anyone who has spent a wet Sunday afternoon in Manchester . . . can read the book and compare the sensations.[14]

Waugh did write the book, and the response to it was quite favorable.

Waugh died in 1966; Greene lived until 1991.

---

[14] Frank J. Sheed, *Sidelights on the Catholic Revival* (New York: Sheed and Ward, 1940), 49.

Léon Bloy

Another novelist convert of great note was Léon Bloy; born in 1846 in Perigeux, France, he was the product of an agnostic, unhappy household. As a young man he went to Paris to become a painter, but he switched soon to literature. After his conversion to the Faith, his life became a personal striving for holiness. This striving found expression in the gospel imperative of poverty of spirit, which he took to include the particulars of life. Bloy and his wife, Jeanne, lived on the hill of Montmartre in Paris under the most abject conditions.

His fellow French convert Jacques Maritain was deeply influenced by Bloy and greatly impressed by his poverty of lifestyle. He first met Bloy in 1905 and, during the course of the visit, noticed that his host's corduroy jacket was buttoned all the way to his neck. In time, Maritain perceived that there was no shirt under the jacket; Bloy was literally too poor to buy one. He had given away his savings as a French railway employee, as well as the royalties from his many books. It was his way of reaching spiritual perfection.

Léon Bloy's influence on Jacques Maritain was deep and lasting. Some of Maritain's more striking theological ideas are extensions of Bloy's, for example, the notion that the saints in heaven may actually suffer for men in earthly life. Maritain also spent two years writing an unpublished work on the appearances of the Blessed Virgin Mary to a shepherdess at La Salette, a subject especially dear to Léon Bloy.

Léon Bloy, a great French convert, returned to the Lord in 1916, and his contribution to the Faith has been well captured by Frank Sheed:

> The truth is that Bloy sees life life-size. We habitually do not.
> As we look at the surface of human action, or an inch or two

below, our vices and other people's look commonplace enough, merely a ruffling of the surface—but there's nothing "little" about what's really happening in the bottom of the soul—the continuing strife between nothingness and Omnipotence. So Bloy sees it.[15]

Paul Claudel

On Christmas Eve 1886, a young man walked into the Cathedral of Notre Dame in Paris an atheist and came out convinced of the journey he had to make to Catholicism. His name was Paul Claudel.

Claudel was born in 1868 at Villeneuve-sur-Fère in northern France. His entire school career was influenced by scientific materialism. Prior to his now-famous visit to Notre Dame, he was first attracted to the supernatural by the reading of Rimbaud's *Illuminations*. By 1890 he was in the Church, and as a Catholic he was known in both diplomatic and literary circles. In the French diplomatic service, he was stationed in Germany, China, Brazil, Denmark, and twice in Japan. He served as French ambassador to the United States and to Belgium. His early works could be divided into lyric poetry and drama. One of his works was a highly controversial, what some would call true-to-life, play, *The Satin Slipper*, which Frank Sheed called the supreme model for the Catholic artist:

> He takes for his clue the Portuguese proverb, "God writes straight with crooked lines," and he amplifies this to read *All things minister to a divine purpose and so to one another.* Even the falterings of circumstance and the patterning of

[15] Ibid., 61.

personality, *sin and falsehood*, are made to serve truth and justice, and above all salvation, in the long run.[16]

Claudel was a great apologist for and defender of the Catholic Faith. His work *Ways and Crossways* brings this out very well. It is a series of essays, each of which develops some particular mystery of the Faith and brings out with wonderful lucidity what he found in it. Claudel could do this because he had experienced a significant transformation in his life.

[16] Ibid., 10.

13

RONALD A. KNOX

A conversion in "slow motion"

For a third of a century, Msgr. Ronald Knox was the most celebrated Catholic priest in England. With his friends G. K. Chesterton and Hilaire Belloc, he was the "third man" of the trio of witty and brilliant apologists of the Catholic faith who did so much both to rescue the reputation of Catholicism in English eyes, and to make the faith intelligible and attractive to their generation.[1]

That was one commentator's view, but few, if any, others would disagree. Monsignor Knox gave us the famous "slow motion" books, including *The Mass in Slow Motion*, *The Creed in Slow Motion*, *Retreat in Slow Motion*, and *The Gospel in Slow Motion*. It is altogether fitting, then, to consider the life of this remarkable priest in slow motion as well.

Ronald Arbuthnott Knox was one of six children born to Reverend Edmund and Ellen French Knox. His father was to become Anglican bishop of Manchester, England, but at the time of Ronald's birth he was vicar of the parish church of Kibworth in Leicestershire. It was in the vicarage that Ronald was born, on February 17, 1888.

Of the four sons and two daughters born to Reverend and

[1] Kevin L. Morris, *Msgr. Ronald A. Knox: A Great Teacher* (London: Catholic Truth Society, 1995), 3.

Mrs. Knox, the sons were particularly distinguished. Edmund became editor of *Punch*. Dillwyn, a respected cryptographer partly responsible for breaking the German code during the First World War, was also a very caring individual, according to his friend the economist John Maynard Keynes. Wilfrid, a member of the Oratory of the Good Shepherd, distinguished himself in the Anglo-Catholic world for his religious fervor and heightened sense of social awareness, working with the poor in London's East End. Ronald, the fourth son, naturally brilliant, was led in his quest for ultimate truth to embrace the fullness of faith.

In 1900, Ronald went to Eton, and though he was not yet into his teens, he began to be attracted to "High Church" thinking within Anglicanism. Ronald's father, Bishop Knox, belonged to the evangelical wing of the Church of England. As a result, his son grew up exposed to a great deal of emotional fervor but little rational thought to substantiate belief. This accounted for his desire to make up what was lacking in his background and, more particularly, for his interest in the Catholic origins of Eton. He discovered that the school had originally been dedicated to our Lady, and with that discovery he developed a lifelong devotion to her. By the time he matriculated in Oxford, his movement toward Catholicism had grown to include an intense spiritual life and rigorous ascetical practices.

Ronald was similar to many converts in his discovery that agreed-upon doctrine was hardly a rallying point in Anglicanism. He searched for a clear theology that was at the same time rational and understandable to the mind. What he found was that not everything about religion could be rational, and upon this he developed one of the major themes of his writings, namely, the power of God's grace working in a person to influence the will apart from the intellect. Looking back on those early years, he admitted that, even then, he "dreaded the undue interference of emotion in religion".[2] His epic work, *Enthusiasm*, published in 1950, examines emotionalism in various religions of the world.

There is no question that, in his college years at Oxford, he felt certain God had a special plan for his life. Undue affection and intimacy were to thwart that plan; nonetheless, he was much aware of his humanity, conscious of "[h]ow much my nature craved for human sympathy and support." He continues, "I thought it my obvious duty to deny myself that tenderest sympathy and support which a happy marriage would bring."[3]

Acting on this he made a private vow of celibacy, took orders in the Anglican Church in 1912, and was appointed a fellow and chaplain of Trinity College, Oxford. His thoughts on the eve of his Anglican ordination are revealing:

> I don't really see my way beyond Anglican orders at present. At the same time, I can't feel that the Church of England is an ultimate solution: in 50 years or a hundred I believe we Romanizers will either have got the Church or been turned out of it. I may not live to see it, but I hope never to live so long as to cease praying for it.[4]

What could have motivated a man on the eve of his entry into the Church of England to express such sentiments so directly? Essentially, it was his belief that the Church's Faith, whole and entire, came from God through the merits of the death of Christ and by the working of the Holy Spirit. Anything short of this would not be divine in origin and would

[2] Ibid., 4.
[3] Ibid., 5.
[4] Ronald Knox, cited in Evelyn Waugh, *Monsignor Ronald Knox* (Boston: Little, Brown, 1959), 108.

therefore be false. Knox never subscribed to the view that the Church was composed of half-truths, fable, superstition, and so forth. To have done so would have meant also accepting the position that some doctrines must be believed, while others could be easily discarded. Knox may have had doubts about the true authority charged with administering the Faith, but a whole body of belief there surely was. Despite his misgivings, he remained an Anglican for a time. Evelyn Waugh, one of his best-known biographers, summed up well Knox' views during his years at Trinity College:

> [The Church of England] was a true branch of the Latin Church of the West, which through an accident of history had been partly severed from the trunk. She was feloniously held in bondage by the State. She was justly entitled to all the privileges that had been hers in 1500, and to all the developments of the Council of Trent. It was her manifest destiny in God's own good time to return rejoicing to her proper obedience. He accepted the validity of her Orders on the *a priori* reasoning that it could not be God's will to leave so many excellent people, who in good faith sought them, deprived of the sacramental graces.[5]

Given that, it is not a surprise that Knox, preaching in an Anglican cathedral, could have said the following:

> Sorrowing she [Rome] calls us like that Mother of old, who sought her Son and could not find him, . . . we dare not doubt that Jesus will be our Shepherd, till the time when he gathers his fold together; and that though we do not live to see it, England will once again become the dowry of Mary, and the Church of England will once again be builded on the rock she was hewn from.[6]

[5] Waugh, op. cit., 109.
[6] Ibid.

Even more forcefully, again from an Anglican pulpit, he said:

> [W]e cannot set our feet upon the rock of Peter, but only watch the shadow of Peter passing by, and hope that it may fall on us and heal us. . . . Mary . . . has not forgotten her children just because they have run away from their school-master . . . and are trying to find their way home again, humbled and terrified in the darkness.[7]

He surely was, then, for many years an Anglican with strong leanings toward Rome. The sacramental system, at the very heart of Catholicism, was emphasized only among certain groups of Anglicans. Knox strongly encouraged this emphasis, and at the same time he sharply criticized the inroads Modernism was making at Trinity College. He thought that this had come about through the influence of the German school of biblical criticism, and that, if it went unchecked, dire consequences might result.

There were intellectual fellow travelers at Trinity with whom Ronald made fast friendships. One was Harold Macmillan, a future British prime minister; another, Guy Lawrence, a brilliant young student who would lose his life in the First World War. Knox's desire to leave the Anglican Communion was heightened in 1915, when he heard that Lawrence had become a Catholic and that Macmillan was giving serious thought to doing the same. Ronald officially recorded his doubts from May 26, 1915, the feast of Saint Augustine of Canterbury. His brother Wilfrid had taken Anglican orders, and Ronald attended Wilfrid's first Anglican Mass at Saint Mary's Church, Graham Street, London. From that day, he was haunted with doubts about the validity of

[7] Ibid.

Anglican sacraments and the reality of what Anglicans called priesthood.

Some time later, Ronald had a chance meeting with Father C. C. Martindale. The famed English Jesuit tells the story:

> He rushed up to me and said: "Can I speak to you?" I said: "Not now, obviously; but come up later when I shall be packing." He came and said: "Will you receive me into the Church?" I said: "Why?" He said: "Because I don't believe the Church of England has a leg to stand on." I said: "But that's only a negative consideration. Why do you think the RC [Roman Catholic] Church has legs?" I remember this clearly, and being amazed that so logical a man didn't see that *not* being C of E [Church of England] did not necessarily mean being an RC.[8]

On September 22, 1917, at Farnborough Abbey, during the course of a private retreat, Ronald Knox made his profession of faith and was received into the Catholic Church. One year later, in 1918, he wrote *A Spiritual Aeneid*, the story of his conversion. "At no time of my life have I desired anything else in the way of religion than membership in the body of people which Jesus Christ left to succeed Him when He was taken up from our earth." [9]

The book traces the steps in his conversion: by fifteen, he believed in the Trinity, the Paschal Mystery of the life of Christ, the realities of heaven and hell, and the forgiveness of sin through the shedding of the Blood of Christ. At Eton, he began to value other doctrines: what he calls the "idea of a continuous ministry", giving clarity to Church history and paving the way, no doubt, for his eventual acceptance of apostolic succession. In his college years, he came to believe

[8] Ibid., 146.
[9] Ronald Knox, *A Spiritual Aeneid* (Westminster, Md.: Newman Press, 1948), 239.

in the "miraculous efficacy" of the Holy Eucharist, the intercession of the saints, the special gifts of the Blessed Virgin Mary, and the office of bishop of Rome as successor to Peter and his unique position among the apostles.

Authority, though, was the stumbling block:

> I could not now find that any certain source of authority was available outside the pale of the Roman Catholic Church. Once inside I should not care how the authority came to me; I did not crave for infallible decrees; I wanted to be certain I belonged to that Church of which Saint Paul said proudly, "We have the Mind of Christ." I was by this time unable to believe that I was already in the Church. . . . Now, either I must accept this fuller idea . . . or I must give up all positive basis for my religion. [10]

Through God's grace he did accept the fuller idea:

> The kindly welcome given me by Catholics, mostly unknown to me, seemed all the more undeserved because Anglicans treated me so generously, and showed so little sign of allowing my religious change to make any difference in their personal attitude towards me.[11]

He always remained on friendly terms with his father, but the Anglican bishop never reconciled to the idea: "Honestly, I look upon the Roman priesthood as the grave of the talent that is especially yours." [12]

Shortly before Ronald's conversion, his father wrote several pages to him, setting out his views on the Church and on religious life. Evelyn Waugh commented that Bishop Knox's views were

[10] Ibid., 240–41.
[11] Ibid., 245.
[12] Waugh, op. cit.,152.

so different from Ronald's that he might have been urging the claims of Mohammedanism or Mormonism for all the bearing it had on Ronald's problem. There was nothing by now that Ronald had not read and studied about the pros and cons of Anglicanism. Only when his father appealed to his heart and to the pain he was causing, was Ronald affected, and then strongly.[13]

Even his brother Wilfred, who went to great pains to express to Ronald the closeness in thought between Anglo-Catholics and Roman Catholics, closed his letter with these words: "I can't say how sorry I am, but it certainly won't make any difference as far as I'm concerned." [14]

As with so many converts, Ronald Knox paid a price for the tremendous step he had taken. But, following his reception, by his own admission, he was a happy man:

I have been overwhelmed with the feeling of liberty—the "glorious liberty of the Sons of God;" it [is] a freedom from the uncertainty of mind; it was not until I became a Catholic that I became conscious of my former homelessness, my exile from the place that was my own.[15]

Knox had a famous quickness and liveliness of mind. The *London Daily Mail* nominated him for the "wittiest young man in England". He was well known for verses such as this, written during his Oxford days:

> There was a young man who said God
> Must find it exceedingly odd
> That the juniper tree
> Continues to be
> When there's no one about in the quad.[16]

[13] Ibid.

[14] Ibid., 160.

[15] Morris, op. cit., 6.

[16] Frank Sheed, *The Church and I* (Garden City: Doubleday, 1974), 119.

Frank Sheed, a friend and publisher of scores of his books, often said how hard it was to outwit Knox. The priest was once introduced to a prominent British architect named Lutyens (who had designed the imperial palace in Delhi). Lutyens had a habit, when introduced, of making a statement that bordered on the ridiculous. He apparently got a great thrill from watching people's surprised reactions. When introduced to Knox he said, "Did you know that if you chop vegetables, the temperature rises?" Without missing a beat, Knox responded, "Yes, and if you cut acquaintances, there's a coolness." "That", said Sheed, "seems to me the speed of light." [17] G. K. Chesterton also was aware of Knox' humor and razor-sharp mind. He celebrated Knox' conversion in a quatrain titled "Namesake", alluding to Mary, Queen of Scots, and her Puritan tormentor John Knox:

> Mary of Holy Rood may smile indeed
> Knowing what grim historic shade it shocks
> To see wit, laughter, and the Popish creed
> Cluster and sparkle in the name of Knox. [18]

In 1926, Father Knox began a thirteen-year Catholic chaplaincy at Oxford University. Each of these years saw a flurry of activity: books, lectures, debates, radio broadcasts, and many journalistic efforts. In particular, he was sought after as a preacher throughout Catholic England. Nowhere was this truer than at Corpus Christi (more popularly, "Maiden Lane" church) in the Covent Garden section of London. For twenty-six years, he preached the annual sermon on Corpus Christi, and these talks were eventually published as *The Window in the Wall*. Most of his sermons were concerned with a clear, concise defense of the Faith, aimed at a non-Catholic nation

[17] Ibid., 118.
[18] Morris, op. cit., 7.

that he hoped would see the reasonableness of Catholicism. He spoke in a down-to-earth style and with a great deal of wit. His theology can best be described as otherworldly: today's very strong emphasis on the duty of Catholics to better earthly conditions might have sounded somewhat foreign to this earlier era. One commentator describes the difference:

> He had little empathy with the social reformer: the Catholic role was to colonize heaven, not to better earthly conditions; and the Church's message has always been addressed to the individual soul, rather than to the political community.[19]

Oxford welcomed him warmly: there did not appear to be any significant reproaches for his change of Faith. He moved into the Old Palace, still the Catholic chaplaincy at Oxford. It is in the corner of Saint Aldates, a very old building, part of it pre-Elizabethan, with a large oak beam supporting it. As a Catholic priest he felt more deeply united with the medieval foundations of the university, which he felt had lost its way for a few centuries.

Perhaps his most famous collection of chaplaincy sermons was *The Hidden Stream*, so named because of the millstream that ran beneath the Old Palace. Also during these years he wrote an apologetic work, *The Belief of Catholics*, that really cemented his reputation as a defender of the Faith. One beautiful thought from that work indicates his mental attitude as a Catholic.

> Where you see men, in the old world or in the new, full of the conviction that there is one visible Church, and that separation from it is spiritual death; where you see men, in the old world or in the new, determined to preserve intact those traditions of truth which they have received from the fore-

[19] Ibid., 9.

fathers, and suspicious of any theological statement which has even the appearance of whittling them away; where you see men distrustful of the age they live in, knowing that change has a Siren voice, and the latest song is ever the most readily sung; where you see men ready to hail God's Power in miracle, to bow before mysteries which they cannot explain, and to view this world as a very little thing in comparison with eternity; where you see men living by very high standards of Christian ambition, yet infinitely patient with the shortcomings of those who fall below it—there you have the Catholic type.[20]

Knox' years at Oxford were not the happiest of his life. He lamented the fact that many Catholic undergraduates did not live up to their Faith, and he could not escape the feeling that if his own fervency had been greater, it might have made a difference in students' lives. A friend once admonished him against too much self-criticism, pointing out that he had indeed affected the lives of many young people for the better. No doubt this was true; countless students accepted his invitation to be active members of the Body of Christ, not mere spectators.

Knox left Oxford in 1939 to begin work on one of his life's greatest achievements, a translation of the Bible. He took up residence with the Acton family, serving as chaplain in their manor house. The atmosphere, he felt, would be conducive to such a serious scholarly undertaking. A bit of that was to change, however, when a nearby Catholic girls school burned, and the young ladies were housed with the Actons. Knox soon found himself giving them conferences, which became the aforementioned "slow motion" books (on the Creed, the Mass, and the Gospel). These books were published in

[20] Ronald Knox, *The Belief of Catholics* (San Francisco: Ignatius Press, 2000), 147.

England and in numerous parts of the English-speaking world between 1948 and 1950.

His translation of the New Testament was completed in 1945. The Old Testament followed four years later, and the definitive edition six years after that. Monsignor Knox made an even greater contribution with his scriptural commentaries written in the 1950s and completed just one year before his death.

In the fall of 1947 he went as chaplain to old and very dear friends, the Asquiths, at Mells in Somerset. He was to remain there the rest of his life, and he dearly loved his surroundings:

> Going away and leaving Mells
> Is five and twenty different hells . . .[21]

He was living in a very traditional Catholic enclave, quite close to Downside Abbey. The setting today is hardly changed; the chapel directly across the road from the manor house has not been altered since Ronald's time, and priests continue to offer Mass there. The adjoining cemetery is his burial place, just a few graves removed from Christopher Hollis, a fellow convert, who made his home in the nearby village.

Ronald Knox died in 1957, following much physical suffering. He had received many honors in his life: the Knights of Malta formally honored him in 1922. Fourteen years later, he was created monsignor; his priestly peers recognized him by electing him to the Old Brotherhood of the English Secular Clergy. The archbishop of Westminster wanted to make him a bishop, but he declined, preferring to pursue the life of a scholar, writer, and thinker. He did, however, become a protonotary apostolic, a designation entitling one to wear the robes of a bishop in ceremony without actually being or-

[21] Penelope Fitzgerald, *The Knox Brothers* (Newton Abbot, Devon: Readers Union, 1978), 263.

dained to the episcopal office. Finally, because of his immense intellectual prestige, he was elected to membership in the Pontifical Academy.

Prestigious it all sounds; nevertheless, he was a quiet, disciplined, spiritual, and prayerful priest whose daily Mass was the heart of his day and whose devotion to our Blessed Mother was profound. His close friend Harold Macmillan said of him:

> [H]e influenced me because he was a saint . . . the only man I have ever known who really was a saint . . . and if you live with a saint, it's quite an experience, especially a humorous saint . . . and he did have a marvelous sense of humor.[22]

Frank Sheed, who published his works for more than thirty years, once referred to the post-Vatican II years (which Knox did not live to see) as "the Great Explosion". He said one of the reasons he did not explode was because of Ronald Knox:

> If I had to put in a phrase what in him affected me most, it was the combination of total devotion with total realism. If there is to be a Christian swing-back to reality, his retreat books . . . could help enormously. One goes into retreat in order to meet two strangers, God and oneself. In his books, one meets them both.[23]

Just a short time before he died, Monsignor Knox went to London for medical treatment. Harold Macmillan, then prime minister, arranged for him to spend the night at Number Ten Downing Street:

> Waiting with Knox for the train back to Mells, Macmillan remarked, "I hope you will have a good journey." He replied, "It will be a very long one." Macmillan answered, "But Ronnie, you are very well prepared for it." [24]

---

[22] Morris, op. cit., 19.
[23] Sheed, op. cit., 120.
[24] Morris, op. cit., 19.

14

DOROTHY DAY

From Union Square to Rome

Dorothy Day was no more than twenty years of age when she had her first experience of jail, and solitary confinement at that. She had traveled from New York to Washington with a protest group that was incensed at the treatment of political prisoners. At the same time, she and many like-minded souls were voicing their support for women's voting rights. At first, the members of the group were merely put into prison. Their solitary confinement followed a hunger strike protesting their living conditions. Years later, Dorothy recalled how long the hours of confinement seemed to her and how she spent many of them gazing at the sun where it streamed into the upper part of the cell. "I asked one of the guards for a Bible," knowing it would be the only book they would allow her to read, "and I lay there reading the psalms by the hour." [1]

Public opinion became outraged once news of such a severe incarceration became public, and the protesters were soon freed by a presidential pardon. Dorothy was quite changed by the experience, not politically, but spiritually. Earlier in her life she had believed that fallen humanity had been abandoned by God, now she began to see the providential hand of God in her life and in the lives of others. At the

---

[1] Rawley Myers, *Faith Experiences of Catholic Converts* (Huntington, Ind.: Our Sunday Visitor, 1992), 56.

time of her death in 1980, the press recognized her nonviolent social radicalism, her founding of the Catholic Worker Movement, and her leadership in many battles for social justice. Unstinting in her commitment to peace and to the poor and the outcast, she became an inspiration for the generation of activists who followed her. More than anything, she combined all of this with a devout Catholicism.

Dorothy was born in Brooklyn in 1897 and traveled around the country with her family, led by her father, a sportswriter and aspiring novelist. She was still young when she began to identify with victims of injustice, and after two years studying at the University of Illinois, she moved to the Lower East Side of New York to work for *The Call*, a socialist newspaper. Later she did a two-year stint with the *Communist Liberator* in Chicago.

This job, strangely enough, provided an opportunity for her to glimpse Catholic life firsthand. She roomed with a devout Catholic family on Chicago's North Side, and these people would often invite her to come with them to parish missions and novenas. Long before she had any comprehension of Catholic belief, she had become familiar with terminology. "To make a mission, to pray for someone's intention—", she thought, "what kind of jargon was this?" [2] By her own admission, this was a difficult and very lonely period of her life. The fact that her Catholic friends had their God, their Faith, and their Church caused her, to say the least, a bit of envy:

> I wondered why they never made any attempts to interest me
> in their faith. I felt that Catholicism was something rich and
> real and fascinating, but I felt outside, and though I went with

---

[2] Dorothy Day, *The Long Loneliness: The Autobiography of Dorothy Day* (San Francisco: HarperCollins, 1952, 1997), 105.

them to the mission, it never occurred to them that I might want to talk to a priest. Of course they knew that my standards were not theirs, that I belonged to radical groups who had a different code of morals, who did not believe in God or if they did, felt no necessity for worship in an organized Church. Yet, knowing all this, they accepted me, on the grounds, I suppose of our common humanity.[3]

Such Catholic ambiance may have been a stimulus. A man whom she had once loved had been a strong devotee of Blaise Pascal. Dorothy now decided to begin reading Pascal's *Pensées*, which, though she did not understand them, moved her emotionally. In addition, she read Catholic novels and a detailed work on Catholic liturgy by Huysmans, a famous Belgian convert. Much of this literature made her feel a person could be comfortable with Catholicism, even outside the Church. In her autobiography, *The Long Loneliness*, she recounts:

A friend of mine once said it was the style to be a Catholic in France, nowadays, but it was not the style to be one in America. It was the Irish of New England, the Italians, the Hungarians, the Lithuanians, the Poles, it was the great mass of the poor, the workers, who were the Catholics in this country, and this fact in itself drew me to the Church.[4]

Of all people, a Communist friend who was to fight for the Loyalist cause in the Spanish Civil War was the first person to give Dorothy a rosary. The gift would soon become very useful. Dorothy eventually left Chicago and went to live in New Orleans, where she began the daily habit of visiting the famous cathedral on Jackson Square. By the time she returned to New York to live on Staten Island, she was very familiar with Catholicism.

[3] Ibid., 106.
[4] Ibid., 107.

None of this is to suggest that Dorothy Day's path to Rome was simply taken by an already spiritual person looking for the fullness of truth. In fact, she had a very tumultuous and disordered life. She had an abortion after an unsuccessful love affair, and, on the rebound, she entered into a short-lived marriage that ended abruptly, then into a common-law marriage with a man whom she described as "an anarchist, an Englishman by descent, and a biologist".[5]

She and her common-law husband, Forster Batterham, had a daughter whom Dorothy named Tamar Teresa. Dorothy's first real closeness with the Catholic Church came with her desire to have her daughter baptized. The catalyst of the desire might have been a devout Catholic woman in the hospital bed next to her who gave Dorothy a medal of Saint Thérèse of Lisieux; it might have been one of the nuns, Sister Aloysia, who took a very real interest in her and who came to her home several times a week to instruct her in Catholicism; it might have been her own reading, especially of Saint Teresa of Avila and Saint John of the Cross. It probably was all of these. Forster, however, would have none of it. Not only would he have nothing to do with religion; he would have nothing to do with Dorothy if she embraced religion.

Dorothy decided to have the baby baptized but to postpone any thought of her own baptism so as not to anger Forster. To her friend Sister Aloysia this was not sufficient. The sister was insistent that Dorothy herself be baptized, and the sooner the better. Dorothy realized that she could not put her baptism off much longer—and that she did not want to put it off. From her vantage point, Catholicism was the fullness of truth, and nothing bore this out more convincingly than the way Catholics practiced their Faith:

[5] Ibid., 113.

They poured in and out of her doors on Sundays and holy days, [and] for novenas and missions. What if they were compelled to come in by the law of the Church, which said they were guilty of mortal sin if they did not go to Mass every Sunday? They obeyed that law. They were given a chance to show their preference. They accepted the Church. It may have been an unthinking, unquestioning faith, and yet the chance certainly came again and again, "Do I prefer the Church to my own will," even if it was only the small matter of sitting at home on a Sunday morning with the papers? And the choice was the Church.[6]

Sister Aloysia continued her evangelizing efforts. She provided her student copies of the *Messenger of the Sacred Heart*, which Dorothy enjoyed for its doctrinally sound articles. By her own admission, she studied her catechism, prayed her Rosary, attended Mass frequently, walked on the beach of Staten Island, prayed spontaneously, and read the *Imitation of Christ*, Saint Augustine's writings, and, above all, the New Testament.[7]

In 1927 Dorothy was finally baptized a Catholic; she made her first confession and received Holy Communion:

I proceeded about my own active participation in them grimly, coldly, making acts of faith, and certainly with no consolation whatever. One part of my mind stood at one side and kept saying, "What are you doing? Are you sure of yourself? What kind of an affectation is this? What act is this you are going through? Are you trying to induce emotion, induce faith, partake of an opiate, the opiate of the people?" I felt like a hypocrite if I got down on my knees and shuddered at the thought of anyone seeing me.[8]

[6] Ibid., 139.
[7] Ibid., 142.
[8] Ibid., 148–49.

Dorothy believed the Church to be the Mystical Body of Christ in this world, and that would always be cause for her greatest and deepest joy. The Church in its human element, however, often fell short of the mark. Comprised as it was of weak, sinful people, it often gave scandal, and this Dorothy had to reconcile in her mind. She found great consolation in a thought from the esteemed spiritual writer Monsignor Romano Guardini, who defined the Church as the cross on which *our* Savior was crucified. "[O]ne could not separate Christ from His Cross," Dorothy noted, "and one must live in a state of permanent dissatisfaction with the Church." [9] In more detail, Dorothy outlined in her autobiography the human element of the Church that disturbed her the most:

> The scandal of businesslike priests, of collective wealth, the lack of a sense of responsibility for the poor, the worker, the Negro, the Mexican, the Filipino, and even the oppression of these, and the consenting to the oppression of them by our industrialist-capitalist order—these made me feel often that priests were more like Cain than Abel. "Am I my brother's keeper?" they seemed to say in respect to the social order. There was plenty of charity but too little justice. And yet the priests were the dispensers of the Sacraments, bringing Christ to men, all enabling us to put on Christ and to achieve more nearly in the world a sense of peace and unity.[10]

Those were her thoughts in 1927, but, as she recounted in 1948, when she wrote her autobiography, by then much in her thinking had changed:

> With all the knowledge I have gained these twenty-one years I have been a Catholic, I could write many a story of priests who were poor, chaste and obedient, who gave their lives

[9] Ibid., 150.
[10] Ibid.

daily for their fellows, but I am writing about how I felt at the time of my baptism.[11]

Shortly after her entry into the Church, Dorothy began writing for Catholic publications, and on one occasion she was assigned to cover a Communist-organized protest march of unemployed from New York to Washington. Later, she wrote of her joy at the courage the marchers showed but also of her sharp disappointment that "since I was now a Catholic, with a fundamental philosophical difference, I could not be out there with them." [12] But that did not stop her from wondering aloud why the Church did not organize more effectively to carry out the corporal works of mercy that the Communists, on a purely secular level, did very effectively.

She eventually answered her own question: in 1933 she founded a newspaper, *The Catholic Worker*, and, the following year, her first House of Hospitality, on the Lower East Side of Manhattan. Much of her guidance came from her friend and co-worker the French philosopher Peter Maurin. Dorothy found much spiritual sustenance in his writings and tried to implement his many ideas, especially his plan to develop anti-industrial communes. Maurin gave the movement much of its Catholic intellectual content and was particularly remembered for his "Easy Essays", which appeared in many issues of *The Catholic Worker*.

United States Catholics in the 1930s, and especially later, in the postwar era, were seeking assimilation into the mainstream of American life. Assimilation meant social acceptance, a climb up the economic ladder, flight from the cities to the suburbs, and a growing sophistication. This goal was lost on Dorothy Day. Instead, with the help of Peter Maurin,

[11] Ibid.
[12] Myers, op. cit., 60.

she concentrated on laying the foundation of Catholic pacifism. Her well-reasoned defense of the principles on which the Catholic Worker Movement was based found expression in the pacifist stand she took during the Second World War and strongly endorsed for her followers. It was also manifested by the movement's attempt to sponsor a camp for Catholic conscientious objectors.

On the surface, all of this appeared controversial. It is put in much clearer perspective when one considers Dorothy's holiness of life, a quality well captured by Maisie Ward, her friend of many years.

> Dorothy Day is a poet and a seeker after perfection. Not least interesting is the record of the books she chose for spiritual reading, liberally quoted from, of the early efforts at carrying out some part of the Liturgy, of the determination to achieve daily meditation before or after the mass that was never missed. She faces all the difficulties, describes the profound despondency resulting from overwork, strain, lack of sleep and often of adequate food. She tells of the immense generosity shown by fellow Catholics. And she gives us glimpses of the sudden joy coming in prayer, in moments of quiet, in glimpses of beauty through music, people and growing things.[13]

Maisie Ward said one of the things the Catholic Worker Movement began to express was an entirely new concept of the doctrine of the Mystical Body of Christ, namely, that membership in that body knows no class distinction. We are all one in Christ and bear responsibility for each other. Maisie said her friend took seriously Saint Basil the Great's admonition that people are "fellow slaves of the poor", and she went on to describe yet another similarity between her own work and that of Dorothy Day:

[13] Maisie Ward, *Unfinished Business* (London: Sheed and Ward, 1964), 179–80.

The *Catholic Worker* in America quickly realized, as had the Catholic Evidence Guild in England, that lack of education did not prevent men from studying serious books and discussing what they were reading.[14]

There were soon a half-dozen Catholic Worker houses in different cities throughout the country, and, moving from one to another, Dorothy bore a great deal of the burden of them:

If you *are* discouraged, . . . others will relapse into a state of discouragement and hopeless anger at the circumstances and each other. And if you are *not* discouraged, everyone tries to make you so and is angry because you are not. . . . The only thing is to be oblivious . . . and go right on.[15]

Her publication, her communes, her houses of hospitality all defined Dorothy Day and the Catholic Worker Movement. People judged her, pro or con, largely from their social and economic vantage point. Patrick Allitt, in his work *Catholic Converts*, concludes that

the movement's greatest impact was probably on the minds and consciences of the young Catholics who volunteered to work for it: it forced them to ask whether their striving for success was not a betrayal of their religion's ideals.[16]

While opinion did vary on Dorothy Day, Allitt also notes that, during her lifetime, the majority of Catholics in the United States did not know a great deal about her, and "many of those who had heard her name regarded this convert as at best a deluded, unpatriotic crank."[17] This impression was to change drastically in the years following her death.

---

[14] Ibid., 181.

[15] Dorothy Day, cited in Ward, op. cit., 181.

[16] Patrick Allitt, *Catholic Converts: British and American Intellectuals Turn to Rome* (Ithaca: Cornell University Press, 1997), 152.

[17] Ibid.

Shortly after his installation as archbishop of New York in 1984, John Cardinal O'Connor posed the question of whether Dorothy's cause for canonization might validly be studied and possibly formally introduced for Vatican consideration. He said he received few responses at the time, and, of those who did respond, two were extremely negative.

The centennial of her birth in 1997 provided another opportunity to discuss the question. Cardinal O'Connor brought together a group of about twenty interested people who had known Dorothy well and had worked closely with her. The proposal to initiate the canonization process was approved by all present save one. Dorothy's chance remark that she wanted no one to "trivialize" her by trying to make her a saint was the stumbling block for the one objector. Cardinal O'Connor took a very different view of Dorothy's statement, however, proposing that she meant she would not have wanted to be what he called a "holy-card saint". She was certainly a woman of the Church, O'Connor said, and she would never have made such a statement out of hostility; rather, she wanted her work, not herself, to be taken seriously.

The Cardinal made some forceful arguments about why her case should at least be studied and investigated. She should be considered for canonization *because* she had had an abortion and not despite it. His Eminence thought her *repentance* for the abortion may have been the beginning of her conversion, and her canonization would speak strongly to millions of women and men of God's unfailing mercy. Moreover, her early participation in groups hostile to the Church and her subsequent turning away from them could be proof of God's grace leading her to His Mystical Body. Finally, her dedication to the poor and her objection to the arbitrary use of military force provided a greatly needed witness.

Cardinal O'Connor also admitted there were potential

negatives. Perhaps her absorption in the Catholic Worker Movement led to a neglect of her responsibilities to her daughter. Also, her absolute pacifism was not the official teaching of the Church; her refusal to support resistance to Hitler was "shortsighted", and much of her economic thinking envisioned a society that will exist only in heaven.

John Cardinal O'Connor died May 3, 2000. Just a few weeks before his death, he received word the Vatican had approved the opening of Dorothy's cause. The positives had far outweighed the negatives. The cardinal was undoubtedly happy, and he would have agreed with Maisie Ward's assessment of the real vision of Dorothy Day, the vision that may some day make her a saint:

> [She was] not thinking in terms of the worker's rights or even "duties" in the social order. [She] had come to realize that in this hour of crisis only the supernatural could save the natural. [Her] movement was an expression of the Christian Revolution.[18]

---

[18] Ward, op. cit., 182.

15

CONVERTS OF
ARCHBISHOP FULTON J. SHEEN

For several generations of Americans, the name Fulton J. Sheen was synonymous with Catholicism in the United States. This mesmerizing speaker, educated at the Catholic University of Louvain in Belgium, began his career on *The Catholic Hour*, a weekly radio program sponsored by the National Council of Catholic Men. From there he became one of the pioneers of television in the 1950s with his phenomenally successful series *Life Is Worth Living*.

Born in El Paso, Illinois, in 1895 and ordained for the diocese of Peoria, he was for many years a professor of philosophy at the Catholic University of America. Before assuming the position of national director of the Society for the Propagation of the Faith, he was named a bishop in 1951. He became bishop of Rochester, New York, in 1966. For ten years prior to his death in 1979, as the titular archbishop of Newport in Wales, he devoted himself almost exclusively to the preaching of priests' retreats in the United States and Europe. Archbishop Sheen wrote some sixty books during his career, was a syndicated columnist in the religious and secular press, and won the admiration of millions for being everything that he was. This remarkable man was responsible for instructing many converts in the Catholic Faith during the sixty years of his priesthood.

In his autobiography, *Treasure in Clay*, Archbishop Sheen remarked that "[a] priest never really touches reality until he touches a soul." Indeed, we must in some way or another touch souls, for "[t]he world is in a tragic state when salesmen do not believe in their products and soldiers are not on fire with their cause." [1]

The difficulty in convert-making, as Sheen saw it, was the very human tendency on the part of a priest to believe he is the one making the convert, when in fact the Lord is only using him as the instrument to bring a soul to Himself. Apparently God's grace touched Sheen with this realization early on, since, when Pope Pius XII asked him how many converts he had made in his life, the Bishop replied that he had never counted, for fear he would take his human instrumentality too seriously.

What, in the mind of Fulton Sheen, was conversion?

> Conversion is an experience in no way related to the upsurge of the subconscious into consciousness; it is a gift of God, an invasion of a new Power, the inner penetration of our spirit by the Spirit and the turning over of a whole personality to Christ.[2]

One of the early stories of conversion by Archbishop Sheen had to do with the 1928 presidential election, in which Al Smith, governor of New York, the first Roman Catholic to be nominated for president by a major political party, ran against Herbert Hoover. Hoover was an exemplary man himself, but there were apparently elements within his campaign organization that fueled much of the bigotry directed against

[1] *Treasure in Clay: The Autobiography of Fulton J. Sheen* (San Francisco: Ignatius Press, 1980, 1993), 251.
[2] Ibid., 252–53.

Smith's Catholicism. Hoover's campaign was directed by a retired colonel from Tennessee, Horace Mann. Sheen was a good friend of Al Smith's, and he would usually have dinner with him once a week. Smith seemed convinced that Horace Mann was responsible for much of the bigotry leveled at him, bigotry that he tried to address during a major speech he delivered in Oklahoma City in the fall of 1928.

Some time after Smith's defeat, Sheen called on Colonel Mann. Much to his surprise, he was told by Mann that other individuals in the Hoover campaign had been responsible for the anti-Catholic invective leveled against the Democratic candidate. The colonel was obviously an approachable and receptive person, since Sheen lost no time asking if he would be interested in taking instructions in the Catholic Faith. Mann replied that the whole question of authority was his stumbling block; he could accept the authority of Scripture but not that of the Church. Sheen reminded him that someone had had to compile the many books of Scripture and "authenticate their authorship as inspiration". The priest then drew on an argument from government, noting that "[a]s the Supreme Court interprets the Constitution, so the Church safeguards the Bible." [3] Finally, Sheen reminded Mann that this same Church had existed throughout much of the Roman Empire before any of the books of the New Testament came to be written. His arguments were effective; Colonel Mann and his wife were received into the Church, and on the day of their First Holy Communion they received a congratulatory telegram from Al Smith.

Bella Dodd was a prominent lawyer for the Communist Party and was well known in labor union circles in New York City.

[3] Ibid., 261.

On one occasion, while she was in Washington testifying before the House Un-American Activities Committee, Rhode Island's Senator McGrath suggested she might be interested in contacting then Monsignor Fulton J. Sheen at the Catholic University of America. McGrath explained that Sheen was teaching courses on Communism and knew the thought of Marx and Lenin well. For reasons perhaps unknown to the senator, Bella called Sheen and made an appointment. The priest immediately noticed she looked unhappy, and when she inquired how he could have known that she was, he said that while doctors can often look at a patient and diagnose a malady, so priests were sometimes able to diagnose a soul spiritually. After speaking in generalities, Sheen suggested they go into the chapel to pray:

> While we knelt, silently, she began to cry. She was touched by grace. Later on, I instructed her and received her into the Church. With Marx behind her, she began teaching law first in Texas and later at St. John's University in Brooklyn.[4]

Surely one of the more interesting converts Archbishop Sheen ever made was not someone coming to the Church for the first time but, rather, one who was born and raised a Catholic, who fell away for many years, and who in 1945 made a formal, public announcement of his conversion, which read: "With deep joy, I wish to announce that by God's grace I have returned fully to the faith of my fathers, the Catholic Church."[5] Louis Budenz was born in Indianapolis, Indiana, in 1891. He was a fourth-generation descendant of German-Irish immigrants who had settled in the Hoosier state in its

[4] Ibid., 256.

[5] Louis Francis Budenz, *This Is My Story* (New York: McGraw-Hill, 1947), 349.

earliest days. He was educated at Catholic colleges and was admitted to the Indiana Bar in 1912. He went to St. Louis, Missouri, that same year to forward the cause of Catholic social justice and to work for the Central Verein, an old German-Catholic organization that promoted social justice and published pamphlets, books, and articles refuting much of the anti-Catholicism prevalent in the country.

Gradually, his life changed. Budenz entered into a bad marriage and drifted away from the Church. He began to criticize Catholicism sharply for its failure to rid society of many of its social ills. Actually, as he later admitted, he was masking his own guilt for leaving the Faith. Since he could no longer work under Catholic auspices, he affiliated with the Civil League of Saint Louis, a municipal reform group much in keeping with similar organizations that sprang up across the country during the "progressive era" of early twentieth-century United States history.

This mentality compelled him to move east, to New York City, to become publicity director for the American Civil Liberties Union. The plight of the workingman increasingly occupied him. Budenz held that organizations for collective bargaining, labor unions, were the only means workers had in their struggle against industrial capitalism; hence, such groups must be strengthened. *Labor Age* was a publication Budenz established to advance that very cause. As the years went by, he continued a journalistic career by becoming editor of the Communist *Daily Worker*. Communism was not an evil movement, he maintained; in fact, it worked for many of the same goals as did labor. A peaceful coexistence if not friendship between the two was the sort of theme Budenz advanced as he addressed numerous Communist organizations. When Hitler came to power in Germany, Budenz formally joined the Communist Party.

It was, therefore, as a high-ranking Communist official in the United States that Louis Budenz had his first encounter with Fulton Sheen in 1936. Sheen had written an article critical of Communism. He began by stressing many good points of the labor movement. Whenever a protest was waged to demonstrate the plight of the workingman, the living conditions of poor people, effects of low wages and the like, there was much that was commendable in this effort. What Sheen objected to was the Communist use of the term "fascist". He argued that Communists unfairly labeled anyone who opposed them a "fascist". To that charge Budenz replied:

Come, come, Monsignor Sheen. . . . Is it not the Communists . . . who are fighting in Germany for the freedom of worship for the Catholic priests, hunted and hounded by the madman Hitler? Is it not the Communists who have opposed to the limit the Black Legion, the Ku Klux Klan in America, the same dark organizations aimed at attacking the right of worship of the Catholic priests? Is it not the Communists who have stood with the Basque priests, not only for democracy in Spain, but also for the right of those priests for freedom of worship? [6]

In his earnest desire to put forward the anti-fascist cause, Budenz later admitted, any consideration of bad faith on the part of the Communists was far from his mind. He later said of his earlier reply to Sheen:

With my present deep distaste at this attempt to put Monsignor Sheen in a false position, there is this thankfulness: that it was this very article and its occasion that were to lead to the jolt that changed my life . . . and made me see the Red cause in its proper colors and brought me back to Christ. [7]

[6] Ibid., 156.
[7] Ibid., 157.

Humbly, Budenz added the following:

> It is no more possible for me to explain how I could help
> Catholic–Communist co-operation by assailing Monsignor
> Sheen than it was to say why I thought I was serving social
> justice years before by leaving the Catholic Church. At the
> time of my departure from the Church, I knew in my heart
> that it was solely to defy the Catholic moral law.[8]

Sheen, of course, was not to be outdone by Budenz. He
wrote a pamphlet titled "Communism Answers a Communist", which Budenz called "a definite and devastating rebuttal
to my queries". Sheen pointed to many particulars of Soviet
life that proved beyond a doubt Russia was an oppressive
society. He also wrote of the five million German Communists who were enrolled as members of the Militant Atheists
Society of Moscow at the time of Hitler's rise to power.
These points were developed so convincingly, it was extremely
difficult for Budenz to go on maintaining Communism was
either a friend of the poor or a friend of religion.

In 1937, at the Hotel Commodore in New York City, the
two men finally met. They had a pleasant lunch, but it was
evident that their ideologies clashed. After a wrenching discussion, and with no apparent warning, Sheen changed the
subject and said, "Let us now talk of the Blessed Virgin."
Budenz was taken completely off guard:

> For those who are beyond the bounds of belief, this incident
> will have little significance. They will not comprehend what
> went on in my soul at those words. But at some time in their
> lives they may have experienced the electrifying moment in
> which a series of intellectual concepts on which they have
> long labored without result suddenly became clear. What

[8] Ibid.

happened to me then, was something like that, but it was much more.

Immediately I was conscious of the senselessness and sinfulness of my life as I then lived it. The peace that flows from Mary, and which had been mine in the early days, flashed back to me with an overwhelming vividness. . . .

The drabness of life without Divinity, the slaughter which science will wreak on mankind without Divine Law, pressed in on my consciousness.[9]

An interesting character analysis of the human agent that God was using to bring Budenz back emerges from his reminiscences:

Msgr. Sheen knows the secret of dealing with people who have broken with the Church. It is an outgrowth of Catholic charity, but it also springs from a deep knowledge of human nature. He was not disposed to contradict me in our face-to-face discussion. That would only have aroused my personal pride and incited me to further argument. What he did, instead, took me totally by surprise.[10]

Eight years passed before the two men had further contact. In 1945, Sheen received a communication from Budenz saying that he wished to return to the Church. Much activity with the Communist Party had transpired before he made his final decision to break all ties with it. Why did it take so long? Why did he wait? "The 'why' of this must be laid to the perversity of the human soul when once it has been led into a camp of error through the delusion of being led by reason." [11]

On October 10, 1945, in Saint Patrick's Cathedral, New York City, one hundred years and one day after John Henry

[9] Ibid., 162–63.
[10] Ibid., 162.
[11] Ibid., 166.

Newman became a Catholic in England, Louis Budenz made his profession of faith and went to confession. His wife, Margaret, became a Catholic that evening, and their children were baptized in the Faith. "To be a Catholic is to be of the Communion of Saints, and to be of God's centuries." [12]

Budenz was truly a happy man; one year later he ended his self-imposed absence from public life. Teaching positions came at Notre Dame and at Fordham, and he became a sought-after speaker at Catholic functions around the country. In his talks he would outline in detail for audiences his fall and return to the Catholic Faith.

Television viewers who faithfully watched *Life Is Worth Living* in the 1950s were familiar with its theme song. It was called the "Vienna March", but it had been put into waltz time. Many musicians would consider this a difficult task, but for Fritz Kreisler, one of the world's great violinists, it was all in a day's work. Kreisler and his wife, Harriet, were both converts of Fulton Sheen, and their conversion came about in an indirect way.

Bishop Sheen received a phone call from a woman asking if he would visit her uncle. The man's wife had recently committed suicide, and he was despondent. He was not home the day Sheen came to call, so the bishop, making conversation, asked the elevator operator who lived in the apartment across the hall. When he learned it was Fritz Kreisler, he knocked and immediately began a conversation.

Despite his enormous musical prestige, Kreisler, because of his German birth, faced much discrimination in the United States during the First World War, and several of his concert engagements had been canceled. In the very different climate

---

[12] Ibid., 348

of 1939, he moved to the United States permanently, and four years later he became a citizen. Some years later, living in New York, he had his first chance meeting with Fulton Sheen, and it was not long afterward that Kreisler and his wife began taking instructions and were received into the Catholic Church. Archbishop Sheen once recalled what a serious student of the Faith Kreisler was: if a reference were given him from the Old Testament he would read it in Hebrew; if one were given him from the New Testament, he would read it in Greek. Sheen further recalled:

> I was a very close friend of the Kreislers from the time of their reception into the Church, and it was tragic to see Fritz in his last days, blind and deaf from an automobile accident, but radiating a gentleness and refinement not unlike his music. I visited them every week for some years until the Lord called them from the Church Militant to the Church Triumphant, where I am sure the music of Fritz Kreisler is in the repertoire of Heaven.[13]

Heywood Broun, one of the more distinguished newsmen in the United States, is well remembered for being part of the noted Algonquin Wits, literary types who gathered regularly around the Round Table at New York's famous Algonquin Hotel on 44th Street to discuss all sorts of scholarly and intellectual topics. He was also one of Archbishop Sheen's converts, and his conversion came about in this way. One day Sheen was out for a walk with Fulton Oursler, another well-known convert. The two were passing the Plaza Hotel in New York, and they spotted Broun in the window. Suspecting that Broun was interested in converting, Oursler sug-

---

[13] *Treasure in Clay*, 259–60.

gested Sheen call him. He did, telling Broun he wanted to speak to him about his soul.

Fulton Oursler was correct about Broun's receptivity. Heywood told Bishop Sheen he did not want to die in his sins (he was not a well man, even then). And there were other reasons why the Church attracted him. He firmly believed the pope was the last moral authority on earth. Also, he had developed a strong attraction to the Mother of Christ, following a visit he had made to the Shrine of Our Lady of Guadalupe in Mexico City.

During the course of his instructions, Broun would often ask Bishop Sheen not to go into a great deal of detail. He did not think he was going to live very long, and the most important thing for him was to be absolved from his sins. He was, of course, received into the Church, and he was the first person to be confirmed by Archbishop Francis Spellman after the latter became archbishop of New York. Broun did not live long after his conversion, and, as Sheen related, a strange occurrence happened after his funeral:

> I preached his eulogy at St. Patrick's Cathedral, and in the course of the sermon told the reasons he gave for wanting to become a Catholic. The next day the Communist *Daily Worker* carried the headline: "Monsignor Sheen reveals the secrets of the confessional." What were given, of course, were the reasons Mr. Broun gave me when I first met him.[14]

One day, some years later, Bishop Sheen telephoned a congresswoman from Connecticut named Clare Boothe Luce and invited her to dinner.

> After dinner, as we got into the subject of religion, I said: "Give me five minutes to talk to you about God, and then I

[14] Ibid., 260–61.

will give you an hour to state your own views." About the third minute, when I mentioned the goodness of God, she immediately bounded out of her chair, stuck her finger under my nose and said: "If God is good, why did he take my daughter?" Her young daughter, a short time before, had been killed in an automobile accident. I answered: "In order that through that sorrow, you might be here now starting instructions to know Christ and His Church."[15]

Clare Luce was the wife of Henry Luce, the founder of an empire that would come to include such publications as *Time*, *Life*, *Sports Illustrated*, and *People* magazines. She was a distinguished author, writer of Broadway plays, and, at various times in her life, a congresswoman and United States ambassador to Italy. The Catholic Faith presented her with a body of truth to which she was able to give the complete assent of her mind, and we can only conclude that an intellectual assent on the part of Mrs. Luce must have been quite exceptional, since Fulton Sheen observed about her: "Never in my life have I been privileged to instruct anyone who was as brilliant and who was so scintillating in conversation as Mrs. Luce." [16]

Clare had not had an especially happy childhood, and her life was filled with significant ups and downs. She was never able to pinpoint the root of her conversion, only a childhood episode of standing on the beach thinking of her own smallness contrasted with the immensity of the ocean. The experience gave her an overwhelming sense of a higher power, the same sense she experienced years later attending Mass:

A conversion . . . is the climax of a thousand secret graces. The convert is one who knows well that God is truly at work in the world. . . . "God does not let a day go by without sending someone or something to seek entry for Him. . . . All the past, sweet or bitter, harsh or gentle, brilliant or shabby, is sowing the seed for conversion. All things are preparations in the soul for the blossoming of faith." [17]

This process, of course, begins with a divine initiative in which the soul is transformed. The convert walks "from darkness to light", Mrs. Luce once said, and there is not a day in his life when he is not filled with thankfulness for "God's infinite persistence and ingenuity in pursuit".[18]

The Trappist Order became the beneficiary of this famous convert's largesse; the Luce home in South Carolina is now Mepkin Abbey, where pilgrims may visit the graves of Henry and Clare Luce. Hers was a fascinating life, as was the life of the priest who instructed her in the Faith.

There were hundreds of people who came to the fullness of truth because of the writings, radio and television broadcasts, and sermons of Archbishop Fulton J. Sheen.

Many of his converts he met and personally instructed— just as many he never met. A young priest visited him in his apartment in New York City three weeks before the archbishop's death. He told the archbishop he had made seventy-two converts in the eight years since he had been ordained. "If I were you," said Sheen, "I'd stop counting." Why? Because it was the Lord's work, not the priest's.

What a prayer of thanksgiving the Church should utter that Christ used such a tremendously persuasive personality as Archbishop Fulton J. Sheen to bring so many to Himself.

---

[17] Rawley Myers, *Faith Experiences of Catholic Converts* (Huntington, Ind.: Our Sunday Visitor, 1992), 16, quoting Clare Boothe Luce.
[18] Ibid.

16

MALCOLM MUGGERIDGE

Something beautiful for God

In the 1970s, the British journalist Malcolm Muggeridge led a film crew to India to make a television documentary about the work of Mother Teresa of Calcutta and her Missionaries of Charity. The result was a movie, later also a book, titled *Something Beautiful for God*. The book recounted what he and his crew observed of her and her work. She was to play a very prominent role in his life and in his ultimately being received into the Catholic Church in 1982. Looking back now on his life, one could say that Malcolm Muggeridge also did something beautiful for God.

Mother Teresa's influence was, however, not the only reason for his conversion:

> It was the Catholic Church's firm stand against contraception and abortion which finally made me decide to become a Catholic. . . . The Church's stand is absolutely correct. It is to its eternal honour that it opposed contraception. . . . I think, historically, people will say it was a very gallant effort to prevent a moral disaster.[1]

Malcolm Muggeridge was to travel a long road before he could make such a magnificent statement.

[1] Malcolm Muggeridge, *Confessions of a Twentieth-Century Pilgrim* (San Francisco: Harper and Row, 1988), 140; also published under the title *Conversion.*

He was born in 1903 in Sanderstead, South Croydon, in England. His father, H. T. Muggeridge, was the first socialist member of the Croydon Borough Council and was well connected with the Fabian Society, corresponding with H. G. Wells, George Bernard Shaw, and other members. Malcolm grew up with the appreciation that Jesus Christ was a truly wonderful reformer who had made a vast difference on the world scene. It was all very pleasant and very delightful, but that seems to be as far as it went. As Muggeridge looked back on his life, he saw the entire picture as one of gradual conversion:

> [F]rom my earliest years there was something else going on inside of me than vague aspirations to make a name for myself and a stir in the world: something that led me to feel myself a stranger among strangers in a strange land, whose true habitat was elsewhere; that brought an indefinable melancholy into my life, especially in its early years, and, at the same time, a mysterious exaltation, an awareness that, mixed up with the devices and desires of the ego, there were other possibilities and prospects, another destiny whose realization would swallow up time into Eternity, transform flesh into spirit, knowledge into faith and reveal in transcendental terms what our earthly life truly signifies.[2]

In 1920 Muggeridge began his undergraduate career at Cambridge in Selwyn College. He chose natural science, not because he had great interest in it but because it was the only matriculation course available. After he was at Cambridge a while and undoubtedly looking forward to a future career, he managed to move into English literature. At Selwyn, attendance at regular chapel services was compulsory. It was a regimented form of Christianity, something quite new to

[2] Ibid., 16–17.

Malcolm. He had always believed, and he had always prayed short, spontaneous prayers, almost what Catholics would understand as ejaculations. Selwyn's organized structure, using the Book of Common Prayer, provided an added, positive dimension.

In his college years he discovered the writings of Blaise Pascal, and they had an enormous influence on him. Pascal's was one of the more brilliant scientific minds of his age, and by reading Pascal's thoughts on faith the young Malcolm Muggeridge came to see that, as a sole pursuit,

> science is a cul-de-sac, and results in the dethronement of God and the elevation of men, to the point that they come to see themselves as lords of creation—a role that either makes them go quite mad, or sink into mere animality.[3]

Perhaps an even more important lesson Pascal taught him was about a way of life to which Muggeridge's own life was someday to conform:

> To look for God, Pascal tells us, is to find Him, and having found Him, we can never again be permanently separated. We may lose contact with Him for long periods of time, drowning ourselves in our own carnality and exalting ourselves in our own pride. . . . [S]till at the end of the day there is nothing . . . but to fall on to our knees and pray, meaning it utterly, "Thy will be done!", in the knowledge that God's purpose for us is a loving and creative one, and that in fulfilling it we are participants in His love and care for His creation.[4]

After Malcolm's graduation, a teaching position at a Christian college in India was offered to him, and he readily accepted. While there, he admired what he called the "spiritual politics" of Gandhi, and he began reading the works of the

[3] Ibid., 43.
[4] Ibid., 34.

famous convert G. K. Chesterton. From these influences, he drew a sharp distinction between the Christian view of the world and the secular, Marxist concept of power.

Returning to England, Malcolm married a young woman named Kitty Dobbs, whom he had known since college days and whom he had dated frequently in those years. Kitty was the niece of Beatrice Webb, a leading British socialist. She and her husband, Sidney Webb, were intellectuals in the Fabian–Socialist milieu, an elite group that the young Muggeridge hoped some day to join. Kitty's mother was Beatrice's sister, and the environment in which Kitty and Malcolm were married did not differ a great deal from that of today. Traditional sexual mores were held in contempt. As a result, the Muggeridges soon found themselves in a stormy relationship involving much unfaithfulness and many reconciliations. The important fact was that there was a deep bond of love between them that somehow endured and that in their old age developed into something profound.

Malcolm and Kitty moved to Egypt, where Malcolm resumed teaching, first in Minia in Upper Egypt and later at the Egyptian University of Cairo, where he taught English literature. In Cairo he began writing articles about Egypt and its politics, which he submitted to the *Manchester Guardian*. The publisher accepted these and, cabling Muggeridge, offered him a position on the paper. He was only too happy to accept because he thought being a journalist was the next best thing to being a published author. Furthermore, the *Manchester Guardian* was a newspaper sacred to leftists and therefore sacred both to the family in which he was reared and to the family into which he had married. Thus in 1930, he and Kitty happily returned to England. Then in his late twenties, he had come to learn a profound lesson, albeit one that would still be difficult to live by:

True happiness . . . lies in forgetfulness, not indulgence, of the self; in escape from carnal appetites, not in their satisfaction. We live in a dark self-enclosed prison which is all we see or know if our glance is fixed downwards. To lift it upwards, becoming aware of the wide luminous universe outside—this alone is happiness.[5]

In 1932, the *Guardian* sent Muggeridge to Moscow as its foreign correspondent. While he was there, the Soviet government took him and a number of other correspondents to see a new dam and power station. It was greatly disillusioning, for, despite all the talk of the greatness of the Soviet Experiment, dire poverty and deprivation were all they witnessed. This and Muggeridge's visit a few months later to the famine areas of the Ukraine provided him with positive proof of Communism's bankruptcy. He wrote a series of articles on the subject for the *Guardian*, and, not surprisingly, he was expelled from the Soviet Union. From there, he went to Switzerland, where he wrote a best-selling novel, *Winter in Moscow*. His experience in the Soviet Union had, no doubt, tempered his thinking. Years later, he was to write:

> The enthronement of the gospel of progress necessarily required the final discrediting of the Gospel of Christ, and the destruction of the whole edifice of ethics, law, culture, human relationships and human behaviour constructed upon it. What we continue to call Western Civilization, after all, began with Christian revelation. . . . Jesus of Nazareth was its founding father. . . . [I]t was Paul of Tarsus who first carried its message . . . not Karl Marx, or even Lenin. Jesus, by dying on the Cross, abolished death wishing; dying became thenceforth life's glory and fulfilment. So, when Jesus called on His followers to die in order to live, He created a tidal wave of joy and hope on which they have ridden for

[5] Ibid., 55.

two thousand years. The gospel of progress represents the exact antithesis. It plays the Crucifixion backwards as it were; . . . in the light of this Logos in reverse, the quest for hope is the ultimate hopelessness.[6]

Muggeridge served as a British Intelligence officer during World War II, first joining the Fifth Corps, and later making an attempt to join a combat regiment. When this attempt failed, he received official word he was under consideration for Intelligence Operations and that he should report to a specific address in London. Once there, he discovered he was to open new intelligence stations on the eastern coast of Africa. Accompanying him, though headed to a different destination on the African continent, was another British convert, Graham Greene.

In 1943 Muggeridge was given a new assignment to Algeria; then he was sent to Paris to work in cooperation with French military security. Because of his work for British Intelligence in the liberation of France and particularly the city of Paris, Muggeridge was much decorated. He was so moved by the experience there, he later wrote a play, *Liberation*, that featured one military hero for whom Muggeridge had the highest regard, Charles de Gaulle. Muggeridge's years in uniform contributed, in their own way, to his conversion experience:

[T]he soldier asks himself a direct question—What does he truly believe? . . . Does he really believe it all? Or any of it? . . . That God made heaven and earth in two separate undertakings? Or that he, one of Falstaff's Mortal Men, when he dies will shed his body, a battered old carcass anyway, and then be resurrected in this same body and live for ever? "Lord, I believe" he wants to say.[7]

[6] Ibid., 62–63.
[7] Ibid., 104–5.

After the war, Muggeridge became foreign correspondent for the *London Daily Telegraph*, and then, in 1952, editor of the venerable publication *Punch*, which had fallen on hard times. When he assumed editorship of *Punch*, Malcolm tried to give it wit, that is, intellectual humor, by writing on politics and affairs of current interest. Some of his cartoons, as well as comments he made about the monarchy, on the BBC, won him the label of controversialist. In the late 1950s, he turned to freelance journalism and television appearances.

In 1967 he was in the Holy Land to direct the making of a motion picture about the life of Christ, and there the real stirrings of conversion occurred. The mystical feeling he experienced intensified when he went into the Church of the Nativity in Bethlehem:

> I had found a seat in the crypt on a stone ledge in the shadow cast by the lighted candles which provided the only illumination. How ridiculous these so-called "shrines" were, I was thinking to myself. How squalid the commercialism which exploited them! Who but a credulous fool could possibly suppose that the place marked in a crypt with a silver cross was veritably the spot where Jesus had been born? The Holy Land, it seemed to me, had been turned into a sort of Jesus-land, on the lines of Disneyland.
>
> As these thoughts passed through my mind, I began to notice the demeanor of the visitors coming into the crypt. Some crossed themselves; a few knelt down; most were obviously standard twentieth-century pursuers of happiness for whom the Church of the Nativity was just one item on a sightseeing tour—as it might be the Taj Mahal, or Madame Tussaud's, or Lenin's mausoleum. Nonetheless, each face as it came into view was in some degree transfigured by the experience of being in what was purported to be the actual place of Jesus' birth. This was where it happened, they all seemed to be saying. Here He came into the world! Here we shall find

Him! The boredom, the idle curiosity, the vagrant thinking, all disappeared. Once more in that place glory shone around, and angel voices proclaimed: *Unto you is born this day a Savior which is Christ the Lord.*[8]

About a year later, Malcolm received a call at Park Cottage, the lovely home he shared with Kitty in Robertsbridge, Sussex. An Albanian nun named Mother Teresa, who had been in what is today Yugoslavia, was doing extraordinary work in Calcutta, and had come to the attention of the BBC's head of religious broadcasting. He called Malcolm to ask if he would be interested in traveling up to a religious house on Cavendish Square, London, to interview her. Muggeridge had never heard of Mother Teresa, but he agreed to the interview, and on the train ride up he began to familiarize himself with her life. He learned that the fifty-eight-year-old nun had taught school as a Sister of Loretto in Calcutta before beginning her community of Missionaries of Charity in 1950. Her concern for the poor of Calcutta attracted many young women to join her in religious life, and the growing number of sisters enabled her to serve the poor, the homeless, and the dying in many of the world's large cities. This work was what she described in her interview with Muggeridge. He thought it rather commonplace, and when it aired on the BBC's religious program, *Meeting Point,* critics paid little attention. The *Irish Independent* was an exception:

> In *Meeting Point* [Malcolm Muggeridge] talked to Mother Teresa about the work for the sick of Calcutta with a degree of sympathy that almost reached personal involvement.[9]

[8] Malcolm Muggeridge, *My Life in Pictures* (London: The Herbert Press, 1987), 93.

[9] Richard Ingrams, *Muggeridge: The Biography* (London: HarperCollins, 1995), 210.

Within ten days, more than nine thousand British pounds had been sent to Calcutta. Such a response gave Muggeridge a strong desire to take a film crew to Calcutta for a full-length, close-up view of Mother Teresa and her Missionaries of Charity. The following year he persuaded the BBC to let him make the documentary. For three full days, every detail of the sisters' work was chronicled on video. Richard Ingrams, one of Malcolm's biographers, describes what happened:

> In the process, Malcolm found he went through three phases: the first one of horror mixed with pity, the second "compassion, pure and simple," the third an awareness of common humanity with the lepers and the dying which he found hard to explain. Each day he attended early morning Mass with the sisters, one of them being specially posted to let him in and take him to his place beside Mother Teresa.[10]

Although he was then thirteen years away from being a Catholic, Muggeridge felt quite comfortable attending a Catholic Mass, without, of course, receiving Holy Communion. The influence of God's grace working through Mother Teresa had clearly taken root in his life. His documentary *Something Beautiful for God* led to publication of a book by the same title, which sold more than three hundred thousand copies and was reprinted more than twenty times in thirteen languages. Muggeridge gave all his royalties to the Missionaries of Charity, and Mother Teresa said of the documentary:

> I believe the film has brought people closer to God . . . and so your and my hope has been fulfilled. I think now more than ever you should use the beautiful gift God has given you for His greater glory. All that you have and all that you are and all that you can be and do—let it be for Him and Him alone.[11]

[10] Ibid., 211.
[11] Ibid., 213.

Other Catholics also influenced Muggeridge. He cherished a picture taken of him with Pope John Paul II at the Vatican after finishing a filming of the Sistine Chapel, with William F. Buckley, Jr., and David Niven in assisting roles. Another photograph was one taken in New York City with Archbishop Fulton J. Sheen, who told him that Christendom was over but Christ was very much alive. In 1978 Muggeridge gave an address at a symposium in San Francisco to commemorate the tenth anniversary of Pope Paul VI's monumental encyclical in defense of life, *Humanae Vitae*. A highlight of his address was one of his stories about Mother Teresa:

> I was walking up the steps [of the sisters' children's clinic] with her and there was a little baby that had just been brought in, so small that it seemed almost inconceivable that it could live. And I say rather fatuously to Mother Teresa, "When there are so many babies in Calcutta and in Bengal and in India, and so little to give to them, is it *really* worthwhile going to all this trouble to save this little midget?" And she picks up the baby and she holds it, and she says to me, "Look! There's life in it!" Now that picture is exactly what *Humanae Vitae* is about.[12]

Malcolm had brooded over becoming a Catholic for many years, yet he and his wife, Kitty, held back. Mother Teresa was eager to see them Catholics, and they were eager to please her because she had given them a whole new vision of what being a Catholic meant. The process, as so many converts know, is not always so easy as it appears:

> In our spiritual lives, some sort of subterranean process takes place whereby, after years of doubt and uncertainty, clarification and assurance suddenly emerge, and, like the blind man

[12] *Christian Married Love*, ed. Raymond Dennehy (San Francisco: Ignatius Press, 1981), 29–30.

whose sight Jesus restored, we say "One thing I know, that whereas I was blind, now I see." This is what happened to me.[13]

His friend Mother Teresa sped the process along somewhat by assuring him that none of his pre-conversion difficulties about the Church were insurmountable:

> I am sure you will understand beautifully everything—if you would only become a little child in God's hands. Your long-ing for God is so deep, and yet He keeps Himself away from you. . . . The personal love Christ has for you is infinite—the small difficulty you have regarding the Church is finite. Over-come the finite with the infinite. Christ has created you because He wanted you. I know what you feel—terrible longing, with dark emptiness—and yet He is the one in love with you.[14]

Muggeridge's specific problems had to do with the human side of the Church and the question of authority. As to the first, it was easy for him to grasp the divinely founded, supernatural side of the Church. When one studied her history, however, and came upon scandal after scandal, one could become very disappointed, if not genuinely puzzled at the fallible, sinful humans charged with guiding her on earth.

> Yet, as Hilaire Belloc truly remarked, the Church must be in God's hands because, seeing the people who have run it, it couldn't possibly have gone on existing if there weren't some help from above.[15]

Muggeridge never explained how he reconciled his diffi-culties about authority; specifically, whether he ever grasped

[13] Muggeridge, *My Life in Pictures*, 106.

[14] Mother Teresa, cited in Muggeridge, *Conversion*, 139.

[15] Muggeridge, *Conversion*, 139.

the concept that all human authority exercised in the Body of Christ is of divine origin. He does, however, shed some light:

> [W]hat goes on in one's mind, and what goes on in one's soul aren't necessarily the same thing. There is something else, some other process going on inside one, to do with faith which is really more important and more powerful. I can no more explain conversion intellectually than I can explain why one falls in love with someone whom one marries. It's a very similar thing.
>
> For me, embracing Christianity is a question of faith not of rational proof, but at the same time a reasonable faith. Provided one accepts the initial jump of the Incarnation, everything else follows.[16]

Malcolm and Kitty had accepted Christianity long before. On November 27, 1982, in the Chapel of Our Lady Help of Christians in the Sussex Village of Hurst Green, they formally accepted Catholicism and were received into the Church by the bishop of the diocese of Arundel (later the archbishop of Westminster, Cormac Murphy-O'Connor).

Saint Augustine had led them; John Henry Newman had led them; Mother Teresa of Calcutta had led them; most of all, God's grace had led them. Malcolm received in the mail a picture of himself, cut out of a magazine, with a drawing of a Christmas ornament next to it. It was sent by a nine-year-old boy named Myles Burke, and on the bottom the boy wrote: "Thank you, Heavenly Father, for helping people to get true faith. This old man has just joined the Church. Bless him and his wife." [17]

Out of the mouths of babes! And Malcolm and Kitty would have agreed, because for them becoming Catholics

---

[16] Ibid., 140.
[17] Muggeridge, *My Life in Pictures*, 106.

was a "sense of homecoming, of picking up the threads of a lost life, of finding a place at table that has long been vacant." [18]

And that was something beautiful for God!

[18] Muggeridge, *Conversion*, 4.

SOME OTHER EUROPEAN AND AMERICAN
CONVERTS OF NOTE

Any discussion of converts must include at least a sampling of
some of the other remarkable men and women, European
and American, who came to the Church from the academic,
literary, scientific, and business worlds.

Academic

Two converts well known for their contributions to the field
of history lived on opposite sides of the Atlantic. Christopher
Dawson, an Englishman from Yorkshire, was born in 1889.
His maternal grandfather was a Church of England minister.
A fellow classmate at Winchester was Arnold Toynbee, who,
like himself, was to make great contributions to the study of
the history of civilization.

As a young man, Dawson was acutely aware that Anglicanism had no authoritative teaching office. At the same time,
his faith was badly shaken by the rationalism he found in the
historical-critical study of Scripture. It is true he eventually
married a Catholic, but his conversion seems to have come
from his own receptivity to God's grace. After graduating
from Oxford, he studied the Bible more closely and began to
look at the life of Christ, the Church He founded, the
sacraments He instituted, and so on, as one, whole, unified

system. Dawson was fond of comparing this system to a tree: the roots were to be found in God, and the growth or beauty of the tree was shown in the Church's members, especially in their spiritual perfection. Allowing such thoughts to mature, he became a Catholic in 1914.

Carlton J. H. Hayes, Dawson's American counterpart in history, was the son of a medical doctor. He grew up in Afton, New York. The family belonged to the Baptist tradition, and young Hayes was sent to Columbia University for his college education. He remained for the Ph.D. and, almost immediately upon finishing, joined Columbia's faculty, teaching modern European history. Hayes' conversion came ten years earlier than Dawson's, and began, not with any significant faith crisis, but with an attraction to Catholic liturgical life. He, too, married a Catholic, a very devout one, and the influence of his wife appears to have made Catholicism a more forceful theme in his writings.

Professor Patrick Allitt draws an interesting parallel between Dawson and Hayes:

> Both received the best education their respective nations had to offer, and both then converted to Catholicism in their twenties. Each married a born Catholic but converted only after prolonged study and meditation on religious life and history. As Catholics they deplored the polemical war many of their coreligionists were waging against Protestants, and each played an active role in organizations for promoting interreligious harmony against the common enemies of religion. They also helped to found, and contributed regularly to, journals that aimed to raise intellectual standards within the Catholic Church, and they were on friendly terms with many of the apologists of Chesterton's generation.[1]

[1] Patrick Allitt, *Catholic Converts: British and American Intellectuals Turn to Rome* (Ithaca: Cornell University Press, 1997), 238.

This conciliation did not for a moment diminish their Catholic enthusiasm. In 1916, Carlton Hayes wrote a textbook for college use, *A Political and Social History of Modern Europe*. He discussed the strong Catholicism that had existed on the Continent prior to the Reformation and concluded that its breakdown resulted in the development of strong nationalistic fervor in many countries. Christopher Dawson was not very far removed from this thought in 1929 when he wrote *Progress and Religion*. Progress, he said, developed after the Reformation, but it was the sort of progress one could legitimately question. Allitt notes:

> Growing up as Protestants . . . these . . . convert historians had learned to value the Reformation as one of the triumphs of history, which had brought truth out of the brutal, superstitious Dark Ages. But when they became Catholics, they turned this idea of the past on its head and learned to look on the Middle Ages as the great age of faith and the Reformation as a catastrophe.[2]

Dawson continued to make intellectual contributions for years, publishing any number of titles through Sheed and Ward. He lamented the fact that so much Church history had been written apart from the secular currents of the age. Dawson's aim, in each of his works, was to place the Church in its proper perspective as bulwark of Western civilization.

Carlton Hayes was a more public figure. He was appointed U.S. ambassador to Spain by Franklin D. Roosevelt in 1942. Though he had no particular diplomatic skills, neither had he taken a pronounced position on fascism. Roosevelt therefore considered this eastern, liberal, Catholic, Democratic professor a safe choice and perhaps even an effective one to steer

[2] Ibid., 245–46.

Spain away from an alliance with the Nazis during the Second World War.

This one-time president of the American Catholic Historical Association was honored by the University of Notre Dame in 1946 when he was awarded its prestigious Laetare Medal for outstanding contributions to the Church. His death came eighteen years later at his farm near Afton, New York.

Shane Leslie is another interesting case study. Born in 1885 and Eton-educated, he was a first cousin of Winston Churchill. At age sixteen, he went to Paris to study, and undoubtedly experienced his first taste of Catholicism at the Cathedral of Notre Dame. Writing about it years later, he vividly recounted the spiritual uplift that had come to him. His life's travels brought him to Russia, where he was much influenced by Tolstoy. Later, he went to the University of Louvain in Belgium to study Scholastic philosophy at the famed Institute opened some years earlier at the request of Pope Leo XIII. While there, he became friendly with Cardinal Mercier, with whom he long maintained a friendship.

It was back in England, as an undergraduate at King's College, Cambridge, that his decision to become a Catholic became final. The year was 1906, and the one person most responsible was Monsignor Robert Hugh Benson. Leslie's conversion was not well accepted by his family, nor was his decision some years later to run for the seat in Parliament occupied by his uncle.

Unsuccessful in his bid, Leslie traveled to the United States, where he became a well-known speaker for the Gaelic revival, that is, the movement urging a return to the study of Ireland's ancient language. At the same time, he championed the cause of Home Rule for Ireland, and he combined this, during the First World War, with strong support for the British cause.

Leslie had been born into an Anglo-Irish family, and he apparently had no difficulty espousing both English and Irish causes. As one commentator put it: "Leslie was Irish enough to resent England's high-handed treatment of Catholic Ireland but English enough to deplore pro-German sentiment among Irish Americans."[3]

Another convert from the academic world became well known as president of the Oxford Union and captain of Oxford's debating team. His name was Christopher Hollis, and his teaching career eventually brought him to Stonyhurst, the famous Jesuit college in the North of England, as well as to the University of Notre Dame in Indiana. Strongly influenced by the writings of converts such as Newman and Chesterton, Hollis also kept up a close friendship with Monsignor Ronald Knox, and he was his neighbor when the famous convert priest made his home with the Asquith family at Mells in Somerset. In fact, one may visit Hollis' grave in Mells churchyard, just a few feet from that of Monsignor Knox. As with so many young men at that time, his early education was at Eton. He was the son of an Anglican bishop and made his way to the Church through sheer force of intelligence, aided by God's grace. Hollis finished his career with a seat in Parliament, serving as a Conservative M.P.

Literature

From the world of literature, one of the best-remembered and respected converts is Fulton Oursler. A versatile man, he

[3] Ibid., 185.

was at different times editor, novelist, playwright, and writer of mystery stories and radio programs. His true genius, though, emerged when he was writing about Christianity.

Fulton was raised in the Protestant tradition, but at age fifteen he announced to a friend that he no longer had any religious faith. In fact, he remained an agnostic for several years. When he returned to a life of faith, it was to the Catholic Church. Naturally, many asked why, and his reply was: "I do not feel that I can tell all of it. There is too much of it that belongs in the secret places of the heart." [4]

His was a shipboard conversion. Oursler and his wife had taken a cruise from Greece to the Holy Land, thinking that in the course of the journey they would mentally recapture many of the scenes they had studied in Sunday school. Once home, he began writing a book he was going to title "A Skeptic in the Holy Land". But as the skeptic wrote, he became less skeptical. The subject matter gripped him with such intensity that he became strongly compelled to write a biography of Christ. Such a work would offer the world a much-needed story of courage and character, and, in order to do justice to his topic, he made yet another trip to the Holy Land. Oursler understood by now that he was no skeptic. He wrote *The Greatest Story Ever Told*, sought out a priest for instruction, and entered the household of faith.

According to a close friend, he was a "meticulous practicing Catholic". The friend was Dr. Norman Vincent Peale, pastor of the Marble Collegiate Church in New York City, author of *The Power of Positive Thinking*, and more popularly referred to as "America's Minister to Millions":

[4] Fulton Oursler, cited in Rawley Myers, *Faith Experiences of Catholic Converts* (Huntington, Ind.: Our Sunday Visitor, 1992), 130.

[T]o me he was the perfect sort of Christian. He was a solid believer both intellectually and emotionally, he was a mind and heart disciple, convinced in his intellect and committed in his deepest inner emotional life. He stood for what Christianity stands for, and he was certainly not given to compromise. He lived up to his faith in all circumstances.[5]

Dr. Peale also saw that Oursler would not tolerate any kind of attack on his Faith. He recounted a story that Oursler had told him of a party in Hollywood, which Fulton had attended with his wife, Grace:

[A] discussion that had begun intellectually degenerated, he told me, into slurrious references to his faith. Finally, Fulton arose and quite calmly said, "Come, Grace, we are leaving these people since they have no respect for our faith or for us." So Grace and Fulton walked out amidst a hush.[6]

From this, and from many years knowing him and working with him, Dr. Peale could conclude:

This man had faith, he loved his faith. It was everything to him. Had he lived in early times, he would have had the stuff in him of the martyrs. He was never a fanatic, nor an uncompromising zealot. He was just a loyal, faithful man who loved God, who had done so much for Him. . . . As a writer, Fulton Oursler was always interesting, mentally provocative and stimulating. He made sense. He was a skilled writer because he had something worthwhile to say and he said it clearly. He was a genius with words. They poured out of him in orderly array like well trained soldiers on parade.[7]

---

[5] Norman Vincent Peale, cited in Fulton Oursler and April Oursler Armstrong, *The Greatest Faith Ever Known* (Garden City, N.Y.: Doubleday, 1953), introduction.

[6] Ibid.

[7] Ibid.

Sigrid Undset was a Nobel-Prize–winning Norwegian author. She wrote:

> A person must pick his way through a whole network of confusion in life and in religion to come to the truth. But he must seek the truth, just as much as he must seek the right answer to a problem in mathematics. Nothing less than the truth will do.[8]

Sigrid Undset sought the truth because she believed the tradition in which she was raised was not giving it to her. It seemed to her most people she knew believed anything they wanted to believe. It also seemed that a large number of people with whom she was acquainted believed Christ to be little more than a good man. She had once read a sermon preached by Saint Olaf, patron of Norway, in which he emphasized that, because Christ was divine, He could forgive sins. She therefore asked herself: If this man were only human, how could He forgive sins?

She sensed that the religious beliefs of a large number of people were ridiculous. Religion is not a matter of a person's making up his own rules. It is, rather, following God's rules. Sigrid was seeking a religion where authority came from Christ, not from human beings, and, because the Catholic Church was the most ancient of churches, she began to seek out the Church's claims, despite the fact that she had been raised with a great deal of hostility toward the Church:

> She discovered the Catholic Church rich in spiritual treasures. She found that the saints satisfy our inner desire to have heroes. We must be forgiven our sins, and Christ gives us Confession through the Church. . . . We need spiritual food, and the Church gives us the Eucharist. We need a spiritual

---

[8] Sigrid Undset, cited in Myers, op. cit., 136.

mother, and the Church gives us Mary; we need rules to live by, and the Church teaches the Ten Commandments.[9]

Sigrid Undset discovered a great deal of peace following her conversion, and she described it movingly:

> His peace is not what the world gives. It is a deeper, different peace. It may be likened to the peace that reigns far down in the depths of a great sea. Good weather or bad across its surface cannot affect it.[10]

Helen Fowler was a gifted writer, best remembered, perhaps, for her novel *The Intruder*. Much like Sigrid Undset, she had been raised with a great deal of prejudice against the Church. She also believed that Catholics were intellectually bankrupt; they were told what to believe by their Church and did not have minds of their own. So she thought—until she met some Catholic individuals who proved this preconception entirely incorrect. In her younger years, Helen had not believed that God existed. When she came to Him, she turned toward Christianity, especially toward Catholicism, after a Catholic friend reminded her that man-made religions were useless. Religion is not pleasing ourselves; rather, it is pleasing God in His way or not at all. She began to think—and pray—that all would eventually crystallize. It did, and she was received into the Church.

Medical Science

Doctor Alexis Carrel was a French-born surgeon who, in the course of his career, won the Nobel Prize for medicine.

---

[9] Myers, op. cit., 135.
[10] Sigrid Undset, cited in Myers, op. cit., 125.

Highly respected internationally, he was a member of the New York–based Rockefeller Institute of Research. His native country awarded him the Cross of the Legion of Honor for his discovery of an antiseptic solution to treat infected wounds, a discovery that saved thousands of lives.

By chance, he went as a tourist to our Lady's Shrine at Lourdes, in the mountains of the Pyrénées. Prayer was the furthest thing from his rational mind. He felt a silent superiority in the midst of simple faith and so much talk about miracles, until he witnessed a miracle:

> There was no denying that it was distressingly unpleasant to be personally involved in a miracle. Most doctors were so fearful for their own prestige, that even if they saw a miracle at Lourdes they did not dare admit it.[11]

Dr. Carrel was obviously not one of those who feared for their own prestige. He tells the story of going into the basilica at Lourdes and sitting in the pew next to a person he took to be a peasant. He prayed for guidance; he prayed particularly that human pride would not get in his way of trying to understand. After he prayed, he said, a great inner calm took possession of him. It really was Christ coming to him, and, very shortly afterward, he came to Christ and was received into the Church.

A. J. Cronin was a noted novelist, well remembered for such works as *The Citadel* and *The Keys of the Kingdom*. He was, however, a man of medical science as well. Born in Scotland, he studied to be a medical doctor there and practiced as a physician in a small Welsh coal-mining village. He saw people with great faith struggling under hardship, witnessed the miracle

---

[11] Dr. Alexis Carrel, cited in Myers, op. cit., 125.

of birth, sat through the night with the dying, and began to perceive that life is more than merely biology. Cronin was for many years an agnostic; as that mental attitude began to weaken, he became aware that he was on his way to finding God.

He recounted one episode from that period in his life:

> Never shall I forget the occasion when, in a coal mine, an explosion entombed fourteen miners. For five days the men remained buried while the village prayed. Then as the rescuers hacked their way underground, they heard faintly, from deep in the collapsed mine, the strains of singing. The entombed men sang "Oh, God, Our Help in Ages Past." It was this that gave them courage. And when they were brought out, weak but unharmed, the great crowd gathered at the mine entrance took up the hymn with a thousand voices. As I came to the surface with the liberated men, blinking in the stark daylight after the blackness of the pit, this great song of human faith moved me beyond words.[12]

Dozens of such moving experiences were turning him toward God and toward faith. He moved to London, where he developed a successful practice. His health broke, however, and he was forced to recuperate for a year in the Scottish Highlands, a far more quiet life. While there, with much time for reflection and sincere prayer, he discovered that he was no longer indifferent. Christ was stirring his soul. Faith came to him, and his conversion to the Church followed shortly.

Business

Alphonse Ratïsbone came from an old and wealthy Jewish family of Strasbourg; he was a lawyer by education and a

---

[12] A. J. Cronin, cited in Myers, op. cit., 27–28.

banker by trade. Growing up, he had a deep hatred for Catholicism, accounted for, in part, by his elder brother Theodore, who had become Catholic and had been ordained a priest.

In 1841, Ratïsbone became engaged to an aristocratic Jewish girl, but, since the wedding was not immediately on the horizon, he decided to take a final bachelor winter in Malta. Continuous delays in the sailing date caused him to change his route, first to Naples (where he was warmly received in Jewish circles, especially by the Rothschilds), and then to Rome, where he met an old friend, Gustave Bussieres, who in turn introduced him to his brother Baron Bussieres, a recent convert to Catholicism.

The baron had the enthusiasm of many new converts, and, in learning Ratïsbone was about to leave Rome (after seeing the usual tourist sites), tried persuasion. For some strange reason, Ratïsbone accepted the gift of a Miraculous Medal from the baron, even allowing the baron's little daughter to put it around his neck. In a further gesture of conciliation, Ratïsbone took a few moments to write out the text of the *Memorare*.

Later that evening, Baron Bussieres met an old friend, Comte de la Ferronays, at a dinner at the Palazzo Borghese. Bussieres told him the story of Ratïsbone, especially of giving him the Miraculous Medal. The Count promised to pray for his conversion and did indeed stop at the basilica of Saint Mary Major that evening. Strangely, de la Ferronays died in his sleep that night.

The next day, Gustave Bussieres was to take his friend Ratïsbone to the train station for his departure. On their way, they stopped at the church of San Andrea delle Fratte. As Ratïsbone walked into a side chapel, he claimed that he saw an apparition of our Lady just as she appears on the Miraculous Medal. Bussieres entered the chapel to find Ratïsbone on his knees.

The Jewish tourist now became far more than a spectator. He approached the Jesuit Fathers for instruction and became a Catholic at one of their famous Roman churches, the Gesù, in a ceremony that attracted international attention.

Alphonse Ratïsbone, once a hater of Christianity, joined his elder brother, who years earlier had founded the Congregation of Our Lady of Sion for the evangelization of the Jews, and he spent twenty years in the Holy Land as a missionary to his own people.[13]

---

[13] Joseph I. Dirvin, C.M., *Saint Catherine Labouré of the Miraculous Medal* (Rockford, Ill.: Tan Books, 1984), 166–71.

BIBLIOGRAPHY

Ahlstrom, Sydney E. *A Religious History of the American People.* New Haven and London: Yale University Press, 1972.

Allitt, Patrick. *Catholic Converts: British and American Intellectuals Turn to Rome.* Ithaca: Cornell University Press, 1997.

Basset, Bernard, S.J. *The English Jesuits: From Campion to Martindale.* London: Burns and Oates, 1967.

————. *Saint Elizabeth Seton.* London: Catholic Truth Society, 1975.

Benson, Robert Hugh. *Confessions of a Convert.* Sevenoaks, Kent: Fisher Press, 1991.

Blehl, Vincent Ferrer, S.J. *John Henry Newman: A Study in Holiness.* London: The Guild of Our Lady of Ransom, 1991.

Buckley, William F., Jr. *Nearer, My God: An Autobiography of Faith.* New York: Doubleday, 1997.

Budenz, Louis Francis. *This Is My Story.* New York: McGraw-Hill, 1947.

Chadwick, Owen. *The Mind of the Oxford Movement.* London: Adam and Charles Black, 1960.

Chesterton, Gilbert Keith. *The Autobiography of G. K. Chesterton.* The Collected Works of G. K. Chesterton, vol. 16. San Francisco: Ignatius Press, 1988.

————. *The Catholic Church and Conversion.* The Collected Works of G. K. Chesterton, vol. 3. San Francisco: Ignatius Press, 1990.

————. *The Everlasting Man.* The Collected Works of G. K. Chesterton, vol. 2. San Francisco: Ignatius Press, 1986.

————. *Orthodoxy*. The Collected Works of G. K. Chesterton, vol. 1. San Francisco: Ignatius Press, 1986.

————. *Saint Thomas Aquinas*. The Collected Works of G. K. Chesterton, vol. 2. San Francisco: Ignatius Press, 1986.

Church, R. W. *The Oxford Movement*. Chicago: The University of Chicago Press, 1970.

————. "The College". Littlemore: Ambrose Cottage, undated.

Culbertson, Diana, O.P., ed. *Rose Hawthorne Lathrop: Selected Writings*. New York: Paulist Press, 1993.

Dawson, Christopher. *The Spirit of the Oxford Movement*. New York: Sheed and Ward, 1933.

Day, Dorothy. *The Long Loneliness: The Autobiography of Dorothy Day*. San Francisco: HarperCollins, 1997.

Dirvin, Joseph I., C.M. *Mrs. Seton: Foundress of the American Sisters of Charity*, New Canonization Edition. New York: Farrar, Straus and Giroux, 1962, 1975.

————. *Saint Catherine Labouré of the Miraculous Medal*. Rockford, Ill.: Tan Books and Publishers, 1984.

Dunaway, John. *Jacques Maritain*. Boston: Twayne Publishers, 1978.

Evans, Joseph W., ed. *Jacques Maritain: The Man and His Achievement*. New York: Sheed and Ward, 1963.

Fitzgerald, Penelope. *The Knox Brothers*. Newton Abbot, Devon: Readers Union, 1978.

Gallagher, Donald and Idella. *The Achievement of Jacques and Raïssa Maritain: A Bibliography, 1906–1961*. Garden City, N.Y.: Doubleday, 1961.

Gelber, Lucy, and Romaeus Leuven, O.C.D., eds. *The Collected Works of Edith Stein*. Washington, D.C.: ICS Publications, 1986.

Greene, Graham. *A Sort of Life*. New York: Simon and Schuster, 1971.

Hanley, Boniface, O.F.M. "The More Things Change, the More They Are the Same." In *The Anthonian*. Patterson, N.J.: Saint Anthony's Guild, 1985. Vol. 59, 2d quarter.

Hennessey, James, S.J. *American Catholics: A History of the Roman Catholic Community in the United States*. New York: Oxford University Press, 1981.

Herbstrith, Waltraud, O.C.D. *Edith Stein: A Biography*. San Francisco: Ignatius Press, 1992.

———. "From Atheism to Sanctity: Edith Stein". In *Carmel* (Journal of the Discalced Carmelites), 1926.

Hollis, Christopher. *Along the Road to Fame*. London: Harrap, 1958.

Ingrams, Richard. *Muggeridge: The Biography*. London: HarperCollins, 1995.

Joseph, Sister Mary, O.P. *Out of Many Hearts: Mother M. Alphonsa Lathrop and Her Work*. Hawthorne: Servants for Relief of Incurable Cancer, 1965.

Ker, Ian. *John Henry Newman: A Biography*. Oxford: Oxford University Press, 1988.

Kernan, Julie. *Our Friend: Jacques Maritain*. Garden City, N.Y.: Doubleday, 1975.

Knox, Ronald A. *The Belief of Catholics*. San Francisco: Ignatius Press, 2000.

———. *A Spiritual Aeneid*. Westminster, Md.: Newman Press, 1948.

Las Vergnas, Raymond. *Chesterton, Belloc, Baring*. New York: Sheed and Ward, 1938.

Lathrop, Rose Hawthorne. *Memories of Hawthorne*. New York: Houghton Mifflin, 1897.

Leslie, Shane. *Long Shadows*. London: John Murray, 1966.

———. *The Oxford Movement: 1833–1933*. London: Burns, Oates and Washbourne, 1933.

Luce, Clare Boothe, ed. *Saints for Now*. San Francisco: Ignatius Press, 1993.

Lunn, Arnold. *Roman Converts*. New York: Scribner's, 1925.

———. *Spanish Rehearsal*. New York: Sheed and Ward, 1937.

———. *Within the City*. London: Sheed and Ward, 1936.

Martindale, Cyril Charles, S.J. *The Gates of the Church*. New York: Sheed and Ward, 1936.

Maynard, Theodore. *Orestes Brownson: Yankee, Radical, Catholic*. New York: Macmillan, 1943.

McSorley, Joseph. *Father Hecker and His Friends: Studies and Reminiscences*. Saint Louis: Herder and Herder, 1953.

Melville, Annabelle M. *Elizabeth Bayley Seton, 1774–1821*. New York: Charles Scribners Sons, 1951.

Mercurio, Rodger, C.P. *The Passionists*. Collegeville, Minn.: The Liturgical Press, 1992.

Miller, William D. *Dorothy Day*. New York: Harper and Row, 1952.

Morris, Kevin L. *G. K. Chesterton: A Great Catholic*. London: Catholic Truth Society, 1994.

———. *Msgr. Ronald A. Knox: A Great Teacher*. London: Catholic Truth Society, 1995.

Morton, H. V. *A Traveller in Rome*. New York: Dodd, Mead and Co., 1957.

Muggeridge, Malcolm. *Chronicles of Wasted Time*. Vol. 1: *The Green Stick*. London: HarperCollins, 1972. Vol. 2: *The Infernal Grove*. New York: HarperCollins, 1973.

———. *Conversion*. London: Hoddard and Stoughton, 1988, also published under the title *Confessions of a Twentieth-Century Pilgrim*. San Francisco: Harper and Row, 1988.

———. *My Life in Pictures*. London: The Herbert Press, 1987.

Myers, Rawley. *Faith Experiences of Catholic Converts*. Huntington, Ind.: Our Sunday Visitor, 1992.

Newman, John Henry. *Apologia pro Vita Sua*. New York: W. W. Norton and Co., 1968.

———. *Loss and Gain*. London: Burns and Oates, 1962.

Norman, E. *The English Catholic Church in the Nineteenth Century*. Oxford: Oxford University Press, 1984.

O'Connell, Marvin. *The Oxford Conspirators: A History of the Oxford Movement, 1832–1845*. New York: Macmillan, 1969.

Oesterreicher, John M. "Edith Stein". In *Walls Are Crumbling: Seven Jewish Philosophers Discover Christ*. New York: Devin-Adair, 1952.

Oursler, Fulton. *The Greatest Faith Ever Known*. Garden City, N.Y.: Doubleday, 1953.

Pearce, Joseph. *Wisdom and Innocence: A Life of G. K. Chesterton*. San Francisco: Ignatius Press, 1996.

Royal, Robert, ed. *Jacques Maritain and the Jews*. South Bend: University of Notre Dame Press, 1994.

Ryan, Thomas P. *Orestes Brownson: A Definitive Biography*. Huntington, Ind.: Our Sunday Visitor, 1976.

Scott, Christiana. *A Historian and His World: A Life of Christopher Dawson, 1889–1970*. London: Sheed and Ward, 1964.

Sheed, Frank J. *The Church and I*. Garden City, N.Y.: Doubleday, 1974.

———. *Sidelights on the Catholic Revival*. New York: Sheed and Ward, 1940.

Sheen, Fulton J. *Treasure in Clay: The Autobiography of Fulton J. Sheen*. San Francisco, Ignatius Press, 1980, 1993.

Sparkes, Russell, ed. *Prophet of Orthodoxy: The Wisdom of G. K. Chesterton*. London: HarperCollins, 1997.

Stern, Karl. *The Pillar of Fire*. New York: Harcourt, Brace, 1951.

Sykes, Christopher. *Evelyn Waugh: A Biography*. Boston: Little, Brown and Company, 1975.

Vereb, Jerome, C.P. "Ignatius Spencer, Passionist: Apostle of Christian Unity". Bolton: Coop Hunt and Co., undated.

Ward, Maisie. *Gilbert Keith Chesterton*. New York: Sheed and Ward, 1943.

———. *The Wilfred Wards and the Transition*. 2 vols. London: Sheed and Ward, 1934.

———. *Unfinished Business*. London: Sheed and Ward, 1964.

———. *Young Mr. Newman*. London: Sheed and Ward, 1948.

Ward, Wilfred. *The Life of John Henry Cardinal Newman*. 2 vols. London: Longmans, Green, and Co., 1921.

Waugh, Evelyn. *Monsignor Ronald Knox*. Boston: Little, Brown and Co., 1959.

Wolfe, Gregory. *Malcolm Muggeridge: A Biography*. Grand Rapids, Mich.: William B. Eerdmans, 1997.

Woollen, Wilfred. *Father Faber*. London: Catholic Truth Society, 1962.

Young, Urban. *Life of Father Ignatius Spencer*. London: Burns, Oates and Washbourne, 1933.

ACKNOWLEDGMENTS

The author and the publisher express their gratitude to the following entities for permission to reprint selections from their works.

A. P. Watt, Ltd., on behalf of The Royal Literary Fund, for permission to reprint material from *Prophet of Orthodoxy: The Wisdom of G. K. Chesterton*, by Russell Sparkes, © 1997.

Catholic Truth Society, London, for permission to reprint material from the following: *G. K. Chesterton: A Great Catholic*, by Kevin L. Morris, © 1994; *Msgr. Ronald A. Knox: A Great Teacher*, by Kevin L. Morris, © 1995; and *Father Faber*, by Wilfred Woollen, © 1962. Reprinted by kind permission of the Catholic Truth Society, London.

Cornell University Press, for permission to reprint material from *Catholic Converts: British and American Intellectuals Turn to Rome*, by Patrick Allitt, © 1997 by Cornell University. Used by permission of the publisher, Cornell University Press.

David Highan Associates, for permission to reprint material from *My Life in Pictures*, by Malcolm Muggeridge, © 1987 by Herbert Press, Ltd.

Doubleday and Company, for material from *The Greatest Faith Ever Known*, by Fulton Oursler, © 1992.

Farrar, Straus and Giroux, for permission to reprint material from *Mrs. Seton* by Joseph I. Dirvin, copyright © 1962 by Farrar, Straus and Cudahy, Inc. Copyright renewed 1990 by Farrar, Straus and Giroux, LLC. Reprinted by permission of Farrar, Straus and Giroux, LLC.

Fisher Press, Sevenoaks, Kent, England, for permission to reprint material from *Confessions of a Convert*, by Robert Hugh Benson, © 1991. Reprinted by permission of Fisher Press, Sevenoaks, Kent, England.

The Guild of Our Lady of Ransom, London, for permission to reprint material from Father Vincent Ferrer Blehl's article "John Henry Newman: 1801–1890", in *John Henry Newman: A Study in Holiness*, © 1991.

Father Boniface Hanley, O.F.M., and the Franciscans, Holy Name Province, O.F.M., for permission to quote "The More Things Change, the More They Are the Same", by Father Boniface Hanley, O.F.M., in *The Anthonian*, vol. 59, 2d quarter, 1985.

Harcourt, Inc., for permission to reprint excerpts from *Pillar of Fire*, by Karl Stern, © 1951 by Karl Stern and renewed © 1979 by Michael Stern, published by Harcourt, Brace, and Company. Excerpts reprinted by permission of Harcourt, Inc., and the Estate of Karl Stern.

HarperCollins Publishers, Inc., for permission to reprint material from *The Long Loneliness*, by Dorothy Day, © 1952 by Harper and Row, Publishers, Inc. Copyright renewed © 1980 by Tamar Teresa Hennessy. Reprinted by permission of HarperCollins Publishers, Inc.

HarperCollins Publishers, Ltd., for permission to reprint material from *Muggeridge: The Biography*, by Richard Ingrams, © 1988 by HarperCollins, Ltd.

Herder and Herder, for material from *The English Jesuits: From Campion to Martindale*, by Bernard Basset, S.J., © 1968 by Herder and Herder.

Hodder and Stoughton and the Estate of Malcolm Muggeridge, administered by David Highan Associates, London, for permission to reprint material from *Conversion*, by Malcolm Muggeridge, © 1988 (also published under the title *Confessions of a Twentieth-Century Pilgrim*, by Harper and Row).

McGraw-Hill, for material from *This Is My Story*, by Louis Budenz, © 1947.

MacMillan Reference Library, for permission to reprint material from *Jacques Maritain*, by John Dunaway, © 1978. Published by Twayne Publishers.

Our Sunday Visitor, Inc., and Father Rawley Myers, for permission to reprint material from *Faith Experiences of Catholic Converts*, © 1992.

Oxford University Press, for permission to reprint material from *John Henry Newman: A Biography*, by Ian Ker, © 1989. Reprinted by permission of Oxford University Press.

Paulist Press, for permission to reprint material from *Rose Hawthorne Lathrop: Selected Writings*, edited by Diana Culbertson, O.P., © 1993 by Diana Culbertson. Reprinted by permission of Paulist Press.

Sheed and Ward, an Apostolate of the Priests of the Sacred Heart, 7373 S. Lovers Lane Rd., Franklin, Wisc., 53132, for permission to reprint material from *Sidelights on the Catholic Revival*, by Frank J. Sheed, Sheed and Ward, © 1940; and *Unfinished Business*, by Maisie Ward, Sheed and Ward, © 1964.

Wilfrid Sheed, for material from *The Church and I*, by Frank J. Sheed, © 1974.

Sterling Lord Literistic, Inc., New York, for permission to reprint material from *Monsignor Ronald Knox*, by Evelyn Waugh, published by Little, Brown, and Company, 1959. Copyright by Evelyn Esta Waugh. Reprinted by permission of Sterling Lord Literistic, Inc.

Michael Stern, Executor of the Estate of Karl Stern, for permission to reprint material from *The Pillar of Fire*, by Karl Stern, © 1951 and renewed © 1979.

Reverend Jerome Vereb, C.P., for permission to reprint material from "Ignatius Spencer, Passionist: Apostle of Christian Unity", Coop Hunt and Company.

Yale University Press, for permission to reprint material from *A Religious History of the American People*, by Sydney E. Ahlstrom, © 1972.